PAT CHAPMAN'S
QUICK & EASY
CURRIES

ABOUT THE AUTHOR

Pat Chapman's relationship with curry came about because his ancestors had been in India for 200 years. Born in west London during the war, he was educated at Bedales and Cambridge and had a short spell in the RAF flying jets. Following a period in industry he turned his full-time attention on to his favourite food when he founded the world-renowned Curry Club in 1982.

At a time when curry was just beginning its meteoric rise in popularity, the club became the vehicle for sharing spicy facts, fun and features, recipes and restaurant information. It was not long before he set up a national network of curry restaurant reporters, which led to his regular publishing of the highly successful *Good Curry Restaurant Guide*, and its prestigious awards to top restaurants.

Pat frequently broadcasts on television and radio, and holds regular cookery courses. He is often to be seen demonstrating at major food show theatres and stores. He is a consultant chef to a number of UK Indian restaurants and he has appeared as a guest chef for Hilton Hotels and Selfridges' Restaurant as well as at Bombay's celebrated Taj Mahal Intercontinental hotel.

Pat is best known as a spicy cookery author. His fourteen titles include such best-sellers as *250 Favourite Curries and Accompaniments, 250 Hot and Spicy Dishes from Around the World, Indian Restaurant Cookbook, Favourite Middle Eastern Recipes, Chinese Restaurant Cookbook* and the *Balti Curry Cookbook*.

BBC BOOKS' QUICK & EASY COOKERY SERIES

Launched in 1989 by Ken Hom and Sarah Brown, the *Quick & Easy Cookery* series is a culinary winner. Everything about the titles is aimed at quick and easy recipes – the ingredients, the cooking methods and the menu section at the back of the books. Eight pages of colour photographs are also included to provide a flash of inspiration for the frantic or faint-hearted.

PAT CHAPMAN'S
QUICK & EASY
CURRIES

BBC BOOKS

Published by BBC Books,
an imprint of BBC Worldwide Publishing,
BBC Worldwide Limited, Woodlands,
80 Wood Lane, London W12 0TT

First published 1995
© Pat Chapman 1995
The moral right of the author has been asserted

ISBN 0 563 37119 6

BBC Quick & Easy is a trademark of the
British Broadcasting Corporation

Designed by Judith Robertson
Photographs by Philip Webb
Illustrations by Lorraine Harrison
Styling by Philip Webb
Home Economist: Sarah Ramsbottom

Typeset by Goodfellow & Egan Ltd, Cambridge
Printed and bound in Great Britain by Richard Clays Ltd, St Ives plc
Colour separations by Radstock Reproductions Ltd, Midsomer Norton
Colour printed by Lawrence Allen Ltd, Weston-super-Mare
Cover printed by Richard Clays Ltd, St Ives plc

CONTENTS

INTRODUCTION 7

NOTES ON THE RECIPES 9

KEEP IT SIMPLE 11

UTENSILS 12

THE CURRY CUPBOARD 15

ANY-TIME SNACKS AND TITBITS 29

TIKKA AND TANDOORI 43

MEAT CURRIES 55

POULTRY AND EGGS 71

FISH AND SEAFOOD 81

VEGETABLES AND LENTILS 91

BREADS AND RICE 105

CHUTNEYS AND ACCOMPANIMENTS 115

DESSERTS AND BEVERAGES 123

MENUS 131

INDEX 134

INTRODUCTION

Although curry has come to the notice of the developed world only in the last few decades, due almost entirely to the spectacular growth of the Indian restaurant, it has been the staple food of the Indian sub-continent for thousands of years.

If we in the West have visions of curry taking hours to prepare and cook, it may be because, when we peep into the kitchens of our local curry house, we see an army of chefs beavering away to produce our favourite curries. It may also have this reputation because that's what it takes to this day in India: hours to cook. At village level, where the majority live, little has changed in all those centuries. There is no running water in the house, and if there is electricity it will only be enough to run a light bulb and the ubiquitous TV. Water is still fetched and carried from a communal well or stream and fires must be laid and made before each meal can be started. Three times a day, the woman of the house grinds pastes and spices by hand and painstakingly builds up her curry meal in the age-old process which can take hours of slow cooking. In-between meals she is expected to work in the fields, buy and sell in the markets and bring up the babies.

India's 80 million middle class, in comparison, have a totally different life-style. Doctors, managers, government officials, teachers and the like, live in city apartments which have many modern conveniences. No long hours at the grindstone for these people though. Invariably they have a convenience generally denied to those of us in the West... a servant or three. It is the resident cook who spends her day at the stove for India's middle class.

Servants are generally unavailable here in the West so we make do with alternative convenient ways of avoiding hours of toil in the kitchen, as yet unavailable in India: the supermarket and the takeaway. Our supermarkets are offering ever wider choices of factory-made 'ready-to-eat' curries in chilled or frozen packets, tins or jars. Extolled as the ultimate in convenience (all you have to do is apply heat), these products are rapidly growing in popularity. Their relatively inexpensive price tag and ease of use encourage purchases, particularly from those new to curry. Tastes, however, can be wanting.

Even more convenient is the home delivery service of the local curry house. A ready-to-eat hot curry is just a phone call away. At a higher price tag than the ready-made meal, but with a greater taste satisfaction, this luxury is enjoyed by the average curry diner once every ten days.

Whatever their advantages, both these forms of convenience curry have limitations. They are made by other hands, with ingredients that we may not use ourselves given the choice. And they cost more than home-cooked curries. I confess that I am an occasional ready-meal user, and a frequent user of our local home delivery service. And if you are too, have no fear, I'm not going to try to stop you from using these delights.

There are times, however, when I want my own cooked curries, but without the penalty of being a slave to my stove. Actually I have a two-tier repertoire. On the one hand, now and again, I enjoy a long session in the kitchen making an elaborate curry meal, perhaps for entertaining, or for the freezer. On the other hand, when I am in a hurry, I have a series of really quick-to-make recipes for all times of day. I have selected 110 of these recipes for this book. Some are five-minute snacks, others take longer. Some are suitable for anytime grazing, others for a main meal. Not all are likely to be found at the curry house, others are quick versions of old favourites. Don't be put off by the rather long list of ingredients in some of my recipes, usually caused by the need to list individual spices, as most of the ingredients can simply be spooned out – very quick indeed! Not one of the recipes in the book need take you more than an hour to get on to the table from scratch, with most taking less than 30 minutes.

Whether you are an 'old hand' or a newcomer, I suggest you start with a single recipe first, to prove that it is as easy as I say, before graduating on to complete meals. But please do try all the recipes eventually. Follow them carefully to start with, if you wish. Not only will you have new taste experiences, you will have the satisfaction of doing-it-all-yourself plus the advantage of knowing exactly what went into each dish. And the more you do, the faster you'll get and the easier it will become. As you gain confidence, I hope you'll feel free to use my recipes to trigger your own imagination and create your own recipes.

But most important of all, I hope this book becomes your frequent kitchen companion at the times when you want a quick and easy curry.

NOTES ON THE RECIPES

PORTIONS

All recipes are intended to serve four average portions. (For two portions halve the quantities. For eight portions double them etc.) Of course, it is unlikely that any four people eat exactly the same amount of food at a sitting. Some eat more, some less – so my recipe quantities are 'average' portions, whatever they might be! If you know you are catering for hearty eaters, or for those with dainty sparrow-like appetites step up or down the measures in proportion. A good tip in any case is to visualize portions. It can be done with most ingredients. Take potatoes, for example. Just look at the size of the potatoes you are about to cook. How many will everyone eat – three, four, five, more? Make your estimate. Count them out, cook them and – hey presto – no wastage.

MEASURES

Metric and imperial measures are given. Because they are inexact conversions, normally you should stick with one or the other. However, most of these recipes have a certain amount of built-in flexibility. Unless stated, quantities and timings can be adjusted by common-sense amounts without ill effect to the recipe. Even the omission of an ingredient or substitute, whilst probably changing the recipe slightly, will not make it fail. So, be as flexible as you like. Where teaspoon/tablespoon measures are given (mostly for spices), use a level spoon if you want the dish to be less spicy and a heaped spoon if you want spicier tastes.

HEAT

'Heat levels' or piquancy is always optional – one person's tolerance level being different from another, and 'average' being impossible to define. So, please use your common sense with the optional amount that I give. Chillies are always de-stalked.

VEGETABLES

Garlic cloves, onions and spring onions are always peeled. Ginger is not peeled (see page 18). All vegetables and fruit except the above should be carefully washed, even your own home-grown. Who knows what has been in contact with them?

RECIPE PREPARATION

It is essential to prepare your ingredients first, for example washing, drying, chopping etc. Though it is stating the obvious, I'll state it anyway: read each recipe first. Often, in the ingredient list, you'll see that a preparation is needed. For example, '225 g (8 oz) onion, chopped' requires you to peel a large onion, chop it discarding pith, and set it aside to await its entry to the recipe when called for. Each recipe gives a guide to the time required for these preparations. If you don't have the ingredients ready, my timings may not work. But more importantly the wait while you prepare a forgotten item may cause you to burn items already being cooked.

If you have forgotten something, however, take the items being cooked off the heat, if necessary adding a little water to cool the pan down to prevent overcooking. In any case it is always sensible to keep a small jug of water ready to cool down items about to burn. Just add it spoonful by spoonful. It will soon reduce out as if it was never there, but your cooking will be saved.

I have suggested using ghee in some of the recipes. You can use factory-made ghee though it's not as good as home-made (simply simmer butter in a saucepan for 45 minutes, then strain it), or you can use sunflower, corn, soya or vegetable oil instead.

KEEP IT SIMPLE

Speed in the kitchen requires order and forethought. It is quite feasible to produce a meat curry, vegetable stir-fry and rice, plus a chutney or two in under an hour. But to do so you need to consider how things work. For example, first turn on the oven to pre-heat during the 10–15 minutes it takes to heat up. Next cook the rice. Then start the meat dish and get it into the oven. Next make any chutneys and finally stir-fry the vegetables. Served immediately to the table without standing around, the vegetables will have a crispy fresh texture. The rice will by this time be lovely and fluffy and the meat gorgeously tender.

If you only want to take about half an hour, avoid using the oven and meat, and make a chicken or fish/seafood or vegetable dish. You can do rice (first again) but be prepared for it to be less fluffy cooked inside 30 minutes than it is if given longer to dry out. It is nearly as acceptable. The stir-fry will take no more than 20 minutes for chicken and as little as 5 minutes for some vegetables.

If you have no time to make rice or Indian bread, eat your curry with a fresh French stick or a couple of slices of wholemeal bread. And if you fancy your curry next day on-the-hoof use it as a sandwich spread cold. It's unbeatable!

On page 131 I give suggestions for menus which take from about 10 minutes to an hour to make.

DAY BEFORE PREPARATIONS

Just because we are aiming at minimum time spent in the kitchen, it does not prevent us from planning one or two days ahead. For example, you can cook a meat curry today (10 minutes on the stove and 45 minutes plus in the oven) and cool it for re-heating tomorrow or the day after. The extra time will cause the spices to marinate which a lot of people prefer in any case. Rice can be cooked today, cooled and re-heated tomorrow. It will be perfectly fluffy and it too will be just as good, without you having to wait for it to dry.

UTENSILS

All my recipes can be made with your existing utensils – saucepans, a casserole pot and a frying-pan, so there is no need for expensive purchases. For those who like authenticity to extend to the kitchen I mention the Indian tava (griddle pan) and karahi (wok). Avoid aluminium pots where possible, the curry's acid ingredients react with aluminium, causing a metallic taste in the food. Even steel can react, though it is slower, so always transfer your food into non-metallic bowls if necessary. Stainless steel, enamel, Teflon-coated, ceramic or glass pots and pans are non-reactive. To help you get ready to cook, and to save time, each recipe lists the main utensil(s) – such as pots and pans – that you'll need. Electric tools have virtues and limitations, especially for the cook in a hurry. They take time to set up and more time to clean after use. You'll need one or other gadget to grind whole spices (unless you fancy the elbow power of the mortar and pestle). And at least one major power tool is certainly useful to purée, shred, blend or pulverize when you have the time for serious cooking. Most of these recipes avoid these preparations so can be made without such tools.

SAUCEPANS

I recommend three sizes of lidded saucepan in my recipes. Small is about 15 cm (6 inches) in diameter containing 750 ml (1¼ pints), medium about 18 cm (7¼ inches) containing 1.5 litres (2½ pints) and large about 23 cm (9 inches) containing 2.7 litres (4¾ pints). A small unlidded non-stick pan is also useful.

CASSEROLE POT

When it comes to cooking meat curries, I recommend using a casserole pot in the oven. You need a few minutes on the stove top to start the recipe off, then to save you time and the effort of frequent stirring, and to prevent the real potential of sticking and burning the dish, simply transfer it to a lidded casserole pot, pop it into a pre-heated oven and leave it to cook itself. Heavy cast-iron enamelled pots are best, giving stick-free virtually fool-proof results. You only really need one pot so, hang the expense, go out and buy a really good one. It needs to be about 2.5 litre (4¹/₂ pint) capacity for the four-portion recipes in this book.

Always clean off heavy cooking dirt immediately after use. Use a nylon-bristled washing-up brush on enamelled pots, never a scourer. Stubborn marks can be removed by filling the casserole pot with water with a couple of tablespoons of bleach and bringing to simmer.

KARAHI, KADAI OR KORAI

The best-known traditional Indian cooking pot, also called the balti pan. It is round-bottomed, two-handled and made of heavy cast iron. It varies in size from about 10 cm (4 inches) to 75 cm (30 inches) and is used for deep-frying, simmering and stir-frying, resting directly on top of hot coals. Small karahis are used both to cook in and serve in. Modern adaptations have resulted in flattened bottoms so that they sit on electric or gas hobs, and lighter metals (such as pressed steel or aluminium). But this lightness has made the karahi less useful (long simmers require frequent stirring to prevent sticking). We use our oven and a casserole pot for this function. The karahi is ideal for stir-fries, but a wok is just as good and with a single handle it is easier to use. I use both a small pan of about 20 cm (8 inches) and a larger one of about 30 cm (12 inches). Whether you use the karahi or the wok, it is safer to use a wok stand on the stove which minimizes the risk of the pan overbalancing. Having a small contact base area, karahis and woks do not allow halogen stoves to work very efficiently (they keep switching off).

ELECTRIC COFFEE GRINDER

The freshly roasted garam masala on page 28 is used in a good number of the recipes and it needs grinding. A small electric coffee grinder does the job reasonably well and is not too expensive. Newer electric coffee grinders have changeable blade profiles and now grind finer than before.

BLENDER/LIQUIDIZER

A unit with many attachments, many of which, it seems, are rarely used! The blender jug is useful for making creamy wet purées.

FOOD PROCESSOR

A selection of blades enables you to shred, chop and make dry purées with this expensive but useful tool. It is splendid for mincing garlic or ginger and the recipe in this book which it is excellent for is Sheek Kebabs (page 46) where the standard blade makes chopped meat, garlic, ginger, etc. into a mouldable kebab mixture. A cheaper and equally successful substitute is a hand mincer for this job.

BLENDER/FOOD PROCESSOR

Recently, designers have combined both the blender/liquidizer jug and the food processor into one unit. It is very compact and is the thing to invest in (it is expensive) if you are contemplating replacing old units or if you are a first-time buyer (wedding list?). Make sure it has a spice mill attachment.

SPICE MILL

An attachment which fits on to some makes of blenders/food processors. Does wet or dry grinds much finer than the electric coffee grinder which you can do without (the mill does coffee too), providing you own the appropriate blender/processor.

MINIATURE FOOD PROCESSOR

New on the market is a tiny electric food processor. It is relatively inexpensive. Its bowl is about 7.5 cm (3 inches) in diameter and it only has one blade type (the standard scimitar blade). It does not have shredding blades, and it cannot do heavy work like its big brother. It is, however, brilliant for chopping vegetables such as garlic and ginger. It also fine-chops onions exceptionally well without pulverizing them to a watery purée like big brother does.

SPICE CONTAINERS

Spices look great on display in glass containers. Unfortunately spices (especially ground) deteriorate quite rapidly in daylight and even faster in direct sunlight, losing colour and flavour. It is best to keep spices in air-tight containers in a dark damp-free place. A kitchen cupboard is perfect. Even in ideal conditions ground spices lose flavour and are best used within three months of opening their packet. Whole spices last longer, but after a year they are better replaced.

DEEP-FRYER

Although one of the enemies of the diet-conscious, the deep-fryer is unavoidable for certain dishes. Pakoras or bhajias (onion bhajee) is one which most people prefer not to avoid (judging by its popularity) and it is the only recipe in this book requiring deep-frying. If you have an electric deep-fryer machine it is safest, having a thermostatic control. However, providing you are careful you can manage perfectly safely without a machine. In India they use the karahi and, whilst it uses less oil, it is not as safe as a saucepan. Use your largest saucepan. Fill it one third full and no more of vegetable or corn oil. Do not let it heat beyond a light haze. If it starts smoking switch off the heat and wait for it to cool.

THE CURRY CUPBOARD

Most of us, it seems, do our food shopping in a heavy weekly one-stop bash – often at the supermarket. Apart from certain replenishments most of us shop without a list, buying familiar items because we know we'll use them, and enjoying the inevitable 'impulse' purchase which the supermarket encourages. During the week we top up with this and that from here and there. The decision about what to have for our next meal might be made when we open the fridge door, but it is largely governed by what we have in stock. And by and large we stick to a well-practised routine of meals which we enjoy like old friends. At the end of the week we do it all again.

The arrival of a book like this need not change things too much. As you flick through the recipes you'll see that the main ingredients – meat, chicken, fish, seafood and vegetables – are all the normal type of thing which would be in the weekly shop. I have deliberately avoided the unusual and the bizarre. Even the 'exotic' vegetables I have specified in a few recipes will be familiar to you by sight if not by usage.

It is worth purchasing all the non-perishable items for your stores. It means you can virtually use this book on impulse.

Each recipe lists all the ingredients you'll need, including spices, and most are obtainable from the average supermarket. If you have a neighbourhood Asian store you should be able to fill in the gaps, and to help I have given the Indian name where appropriate. Visiting an Asian store is fun. But for most of us, there isn't one that close. All the spices used in this book can also be obtained by post in sensible quantities (see page 25).

Here are some user notes on special ingredients. For convenience I have divided them into perishable and non-perishable items and dry spices.

PERISHABLE ITEMS

These include some exotic vegetables, the herbs and one fruit special to curry. They will only keep for a few days, in a cold environment such as the fridge, so should only be purchased when you plan to use them.

AUBERGINE OR EGG PLANT

Aubergine comes in a variety of shapes, sizes and colours. Known also as egg plant (there are some the size and shape of hen's eggs), the one we need for Indian cooking is club-shaped, deep shiny purple in colour with no wrinkles, and between 10 cm (4 inches) and about 20 cm (8 inches) length. Called brinjal in most Indian languages, it should be cooked as soon after it is cut (and seeds and central pith discarded) as possible to prevent discolouring.

BASIL

One kind of basil is very popular in Thai cooking. Our basil is slightly different, but it is delightful none the less and it can be used in a number of the recipes if coriander is unavailable.

CHILLIES

There are many types of chilli. The variety used for Indian cooking is the cayenne. It is long (up to 10 cm/4 inches) and thin and green or red. It has little pith and few seeds. I never bother to de-seed them but you can if you wish. Cayennes are quite hot as chillies go. So take care in their chopping. Don't touch your eyes afterwards and scrub your hands thoroughly. Many supermarkets sell milder chillies which are stubbier, pithier and have more seeds than cayennes. Called African snub or Jalapeño they will do if there is nothing else available. Discard their pith and seeds though. To locate cayennes in a chilli-free area, ask your local Indian restaurant who supplies them (or buy some direct from them).

CORIANDER LEAF

The most prevalent Indian spice, being used in seed (see later), root and leaf form. The roots are too bitter for the non-Indian palate. The leaves are India's most widely used herb, but the musky flavour is an acquired taste. It is used in the later stage of cooking in many recipes, and as a garnish. Readily available now, in bunches, it does not last very long and loses its subtle flavour if frozen. Grinding excess leaves and soft stalks into chutney (see page 115) is one solution. Buying the (rather expensive) potted version is another. You can pluck leaves as required.

It is easy to grow yourself – but you must buy the correct seeds. Flat-leafed parsley resembles coriander but lacks its distinguishing flavour.

MANGO

There are many species of mango. Some are small, green and hard. These are ideal for pickling, being quite sour. It is the larger mango, skin colour green with yellow or red hues, which gives bright gold, soft and sweet fruit. They should be firm and unblemished, but should yield slightly to gentle squeezing. Then they are ripe and ready.

MINT

There is nothing like fresh mint. It grows prolifically and is relatively easy to obtain year round. Spearmint gives the best flavour in my opinion. If you cannot get fresh mint it can be omitted from the recipe without affecting it too much.

OKRA

Also called ladies fingers or bindi they look like ribbed green chillies, with a point at one end and a stalk at the other. There the resemblance ends. They are not hot and are not everyone's favourite, partly because they can go sappy and slimy if overcooked or cooked too early. Actually given a quick pan-fry and eaten soon after cooking they are really delicious (see page 93).

LONG-LIFE PERISHABLE VEGETABLES

The three major curry flavouring vegetables are garlic, ginger and onion. They all grow underground and they all can last, if you have bought good produce to start with, for weeks or months.

GARLIC

I used to love buying long strings of garlics and hanging them up in the kitchen. It might have kept the vampires at bay. Unfortunately I found that garlic cloves dry and turn to powder if left too long. So, it is advisable to check a whole bulb. Press each clove gently. It should feel firm and not yield. I find you can peel garlics in advance and they will keep in an air-tight jar for a week or so. Chop, crush or press when needed for cooking. Garlic presses are labour saving (apart from their cleaning).

GINGER

Fresh ginger should be plump, blond-skinned with a lustrous sheen and not withered. It would be nice to be able to cut your ginger in half to inspect before purchase. It should be firm, yet juicy. It should not be hard and stringy. Above all, it should be a creamy lemony colour and not have a hint of blue in it. If it does take it back and exchange for new ginger. Blue means it is going off. Uncut, ginger will keep in a dark dry place for weeks, even months. To use it, cut off as much as you need. Recipes call for, say a 1 cm ($\frac{1}{2}$ inch) cube of ginger. Use your judgement for this. It will not need to be precise and a little more or little less ginger won't harm the overall recipe.

Finally, I never bother to peel the ginger. Just cut off the dry scars. The peel will not affect taste. It is really minimal in terms of surface area. It saves a lot of time too.

ONION

Onions are important to curry cooking to create texture and taste. I find large onions are best. Those around 7.5 to 9 cm (3 to 3½ inches) in diameter and weighing around 225 g (8 oz) are quick enough to peel and chop and one is just right for a four-portion curry. Onions keep for ages, unpeeled and uncut, but once they start sprouting they are past it!

NON-PERISHABLE ITEMS

These are the items such as spices, rice, flour, lentils and oil which you can keep in dry storage for a long time. Nothing lasts for ever, of course, so it is best to buy little and often. As they don't cost that much, it is worth purchasing all these items for your cupboard. That way you can virtually use this book on impulse.

FLOUR

Gram flour or besan This is a gorgeous fine, blond-coloured flour made from gram lentils (chana dhal). It is sometimes used to thicken soups and to make dumplings. The only recipe in this book which calls for gram flour is onion bhajia (page 31). No other flour can substitute – nothing else tastes the same. If, like everyone else, you adore onion bhajias, you must buy at least a 450 g (1 lb) bag of gram flour. Store as you do spices, transferring the flour to an air-tight container and keeping it in a dry dark cupboard. Use within six months of purchase. Just occasionally gram flour can go 'off'. It goes bitter and tastes really unpleasant usually because it is very old, so check the manufacturer's use-by date carefully before buying.

Strong white plain flour This has more gluten than ordinary plain wheat flour and is best for naan breads. Have at least one bag in stock if you like naans.

Chapati flour or ata Pronounced 'arta', chapati flour is very finely milled, high-gluten wholewheat brown flour. You can get away with wholemeal flour, but the result will be coarser and heavier. It is worth locating the real thing and having at least a 1 kg (2¼ lb) bag in stock.

LENTILS

There are a number of lentil types available. They are seeds which when dried will stay preserved virtually indefinitely. Because they cook quickly I have only specified the common 'red split lentil' or massoor (which perversely is orange in colour when its brown skin is polished off, but which becomes dark yellow when cooked). Pack size is often a little large (minimum 450 g/1 lb) whereas a serving for four needs only 200–225 g (7–8 oz) as an accompaniment. Keep the lentils in their packet until needed. Pick right through them to remove grit particles which can be present. Store excess in an air-tight container.

OILS

Olive oil and butter are totally unsuitable for curries. The former has too strong a taste and the latter burns too easily. Ghee is equally saturated but its flavour is wasted on any dish involving prolonged cooking. Home-made ghee is unbeatable in rice dishes and is easily made (you simply simmer 1 lb butter for 45 minutes in a saucepan, then strain it). Factory-made is not as good but it still enhances rice dishes. Butter ghee has more flavour than vegetable ghee, the latter being hydrogenized vegetable oil. For day-to-day curry cooking I like to use a light oil such as sunflower oil which is readily available. Corn, soya or vegetable oils are equally suitable. In certain recipes where the flavour of the oil really counts, I have specified other special oils such as pistachio, walnut, mustard blend and sesame oils.

RICE

The very best rice to use to accompany curries is basmati. It cooks quickly into fluffy, flavourful and satisfying long-grained rice. Avoid cheap basmati rice. It is usually not as clean nor as good as well-known brands. Keep your rice in its packaging until needed. Once the packets are opened keep the excess rice in an air-tight container and it will last for a very long time.

TINNED ITEMS

Italian tinned plum tomatoes have a superb flavour and are already skinned, and I have suggested their use in some recipes. In other recipes, where tinned ingredients save time I have specified their use. For example, tinned chick peas save a twelve-hour soak and an hour cooking and their liquid is good too. Other useful tins in the curry cupboard are sweetcorn and mixed vegetables. Red kidney beans are very good too (though it is better to discard their liquid).

COCONUT

I have used factory-prepared coconut in four forms in this book. I have deliberately avoided fresh whole coconut, only because it is hard work and time-consuming to prepare.

Coconut milk powder Widely available, I like this dry powder very much because it will store for months, once its packet is opened, like a spice. It tastes excellent and it is easy to use especially where small quantities are involved. Simply add it straight into the cooking (no need to reconstitute it first with water) as the recipes direct.

Coconut milk, tinned An excellent product but once the tin is opened it really must be used at once. So I have confined its use to recipes which need a lot of coconut milk and use the entire tinful.

Desiccated coconut Useful here and there. It keeps like a whole spice but be careful when you buy it that you get unsweetened (not sweetened) desiccated coconut.

Creamed coconut block Again, useful here and there. It is freshly ground coconut suspended in coconut oil which is quite rich, so a little goes a long way. The block weighs 200 g (7 oz) and with about 30 g–50 g (1¼–2 oz) going a long way, it will last you some time. Keep covered in the fridge like butter.

SPICES

WHOLE SPICES

Spices are vegetable matter, such as seeds, pods, leaves, bark, buds, flowers and even tree resin. It is their natural oils which create their flavours, and these are 'held' within the spice following a short drying period after they are cropped. In this dried, whole form, spices can last for years. Usually they are sold in clear packets or jars enabling you to inspect them. They should look vibrant bright and lustrous. Dull colours and limp, wrinkled spices should be rejected. And watch out for little holes. Just occasionally they occur and it means weevils are present. They are tiny black round bettles, harmless enough but hard to get rid of if they take up residence in your kitchen.

Transfer the spices to containers (see page 14) and use as required.

Here are all the whole spices which are used in this book. I recommend you buy all of them. They will not cost that much. The star rating indicates whether the particular spice is used a lot in this book or not. Three stars means used in a lot of recipes, one star means a few recipes. Indian (Hindi) names are also given.

BAY LEAF tej patia ***

A favourite in British cooking, the bay leaf is just as good for giving fragrance in some subtle curry and rice dishes. Nice to suck but not to eat.

CARDAMOM, BROWN OR BLACK burra elaichi *

Large, oval, hairy, chocolate brown pods containing black, somewhat sticky, seeds. It has a more 'astringent' flavour than green cardamom and is used whole (pod and all) in garam masala and certain curries. Serve the pod with the food it's cooked in, but don't eat it.

CARDAMOM, GREEN harra elaichi ***

Smaller and more delicate in flavour than the brown version, the green cardamom is used in many fragrant savoury dishes, and the ground seeds are used as the prime spice in Indian desserts. Used whole, served with the food it's cooked in. The seeds are nice to eat but discard the pod.

CHILLI lal mirch *

There are many sizes and varieties of chilli and many heat levels. Dried chillies range in colour from brick red to liver red but that does not give the clue to their heat level. Manufacturers have become more aware of the difference and generally now mark the packets of the most powerful 'extra hot'. All (but the stalks) edible for those who can take it.

CLOVE lavang **

We're all familiar with the dark brown spice the Romans thought resembled a nail (*clavus*) but less aware that it is a tiny unopened flower bud. Its gorgeous flavour is put to good use in garam masala and other recipes. When you come across it on your plate it is nice to suck, although the woody bits are inedible.

CORIANDER dhania ***

Curry wouldn't be curry without coriander seeds. They are the most prevalently used spice. Lightly roasted or fried, the whole edible seeds give a delightful sweet freshness to certain dishes and of course they are the staple spice of garam masala.

CUMIN, BLACK kala jeera *

A little-used spice, black cumin resembles caraway in looks but not taste. It is quite astringent so a little goes a long way. Frying it first makes it sweeter, and an ideal edible spice for rice dishes.

CUMIN, WHITE jeera ***

Another major spice in Indian cooking, white cumin is in fact a kind of khaki green. Its taste is distinctly savoury, but used in excess it can predominate. Some recipes require cumin to be fried, others dry 'roasted' and both give different, delicious edible results.

CINNAMON dalchini chino *

This is a pencil-shaped pale brown rolled bark, called a quill. It is highly fragrant giving a mouthwatering sweetness to savoury cooking, and in Indian tea or coffee. See also cassia below. Good to suck, but otherwise inedible.

CASSIA BARK dalchini *

This is dark brown strips of tree bark. Often misnamed cinnamon (to which it is related) on spice packets, it has a similar sweet and delicious flavour. Cassia is more robust than cinnamon, though you'll need a little more of it to create the same amount of flavour. In my recipes I refer to, for example, a 5 cm (2 inch) piece of cassia. It is length, not thickness, which is referred to and it is only a common sense approximation.

Several small pieces will be required and more rather than less won't hurt. Serve the bark with the food it is cooked in. Good for sucking but can't be eaten.

FENNEL soonf ***

Edible seeds, slightly larger than those of white cumin and greener, and one of the more aromatic. With a flavour resembling aniseed, which there is no need to stock. Fennel seeds are quite widely used.

FENUGREEK methi *

Fenugreek is used in seed and leaf form. The edible seeds are little, irregular shaped ochre-yellow nuggets with a smell of curry. They pack a rather bitter punch if too many are used. The dried leaves are very pungent and savoury. They need the loose hard stalks removing.

LOVAGE ajwain *

Tiny round edible seeds with a distinctive slightly musky flavour, used in a few recipes.

MACE javitri ***

Mace is the tendril which grows outside the nutmeg seed. It has a similar, more delicate, flavour to nutmeg and is easier to grind. It is used in garam masala and occasionally whole in certain fragrant dishes, in which form it is inedible.

MUSTARD rai **

Tiny dark brown seeds (not black) are the ones used in Indian cooking, especially in the south. Their inherently bitter taste converts to sweet (not hot) when fried or roasted when they are a joy to eat.

NUTMEG jaifal *

Keep one in a grater for fresh aromatic sprinklings over Indian desserts.

PEPPER, BLACK kala mirch *

The familiar berries which go black and shrivelled and are edible and pungently aromatic, whole or ground, have always been important to Indian cooking.

SAFFRON zafran or kasar *

The most expensive spice and an acquired taste, saffron strands give colour, fragrance and flavour to Indian cooking. Wasted in dishes requiring long cooking (it loses its subtlety), 20 or 30 strands (about 0.5 g) all edible, are what you need to create magic in rice dishes or desserts. Although it is customary to soak the strands in milk to 'release' the colour, I have found this is unnecessary. Simply add when the recipes say and leave time to do the rest.

STAR ANISE chakra phool *

A Chinese spice used only in the northern parts of the subcontinent which share their border with Tibet. It is, however, beautiful in appearance and sumptuous in flavour (which resembles aniseed). For these reasons two or three should be used in some rice dishes, for example. Serve with the food though it is inedible.

WILD ONION SEEDS kalonji *

Tiny, coal-black edible nuggets, also called nigella, and neither related to nor tasting of onion. Rather, they are strikingly aromatic with a role to play in naan bread and many other recipes.

GROUND SPICES

All ground spices start life as whole spices. Except for the green cardamom, the spices, listed below are best done in the factory. Home equipment isn't powerful enough to do it.

GREEN CARDAMOM hare elaichi *

Used in the desserts chapter and very important too. You can buy ground cardamom powder, but it will most likely be ground brown/black cardamoms, which is less subtle in flavour (and cheaper). It is more reliable (and not difficult) to grind your own (see page 26). 'Roast' the whole green cardamoms (see page 21), then grind the whole thing and sieve off the husks.

GROUND CINNAMON dalchini ***

Needed for the garam masala recipe, page 28.

GROUND CLOVE lavang ***

Needed for the garam masala recipe, page 28.

GROUND CORIANDER dhania ***

As with the seeds, the power, too, is India's most prolifically used spice. Factory ground is suitable for most uses, but you can roast and grind your own coriander powder (see page 26) for a more 'mature' taste.

GROUND CUMIN jeera ***

Important in many recipes, ground cumin gives savoury tastes. Again you can roast and grind your own for a more rounded taste.

GROUND GARLIC POWDER ***

Used in the curry paste recipe, page 27.

MANGO POWDER amchur *

Factory-ground from dried mango flesh the fine powder is grey in colour. It is used in several recipes to give sour tastes.

PAPRIKA ***

No Hindi name because, until recently, it was not used in India. But good-quality Hungarian mild paprika has a unique savoury flavour and gives a gorgeous red colour without the heat of chilli powder. There are cheaper paprikas which lack these flavours and paprika can 'turn' sour (when it should be binned). So buy little and often.

TAMARIND POWDER imli *

A relatively new product. A teaspoon or so can be used as required making it a practicable alternative to the long-winded process of making tamarind purée. One drawback is that it is freeze-dried so must be kept very dry otherwise it absorbs water in the air and goes solid.

TURMERIC haldi ***

The familiar fine yellow powder is factory-ground from very hard dried roots vaguely resembling ginger. It is turmeric which gives curry its characteristic golden colour. Only a relatively small amount is needed to do its job. Too much gives a bitter taste.

INGREDIENTS BY MAIL ORDER

For information please write to this address, enclosing an SAE: Pat Chapman, BBC Quick & Easy Curries, PO Box 7, Haslemere, Surrey GU27 1EP.

STORING SPICES

Whole spices retain their flavours longer than ground, for a year or more. Ground spices give off a stronger aroma than whole and of course this means their storage life is shorter. Three months from the moment they come out of their packaging is about right for most ground items. Buy in small frequent batches. The ultra-violet in daylight, especially direct sunlight, causes spices to fade and lose flavour rapidly. Keep them in airtight containers in a dark cupboard, and resist the temptation to display them in those alluring jars.

USING SPICES

The secret of success in cooking curry lies in the correct usage of spices. Locked inside them all is their volatile or essential oil or flavouring. We need to know how to release those oils into our cooking. Actually it is easy and rewarding and it takes virtually no time at all to do. There are two main methods. Frying and 'roasting'. Frying is used for both whole and ground spices, allowing their oils to be released into the cooking oil. The process is described in each relevant recipe. Whole spices can be 'roasted', until their oils vaporize.

ROASTING AND GRINDING YOUR OWN SPICES

The simplest way to 'roast' spices is to stir-fry them in a hot, dry wok. Coriander or cumin seeds benefit greatly from this process, releasing wonderful aromas (their oils). They can be used in subsequent cooking or cooled and stored in an air-tight jar, although it is quick enough to make to order, so to speak and better, with no loss of flavour in storage. Following roasting, if you intend to grind the spice, allow it first to cool. Then grind it in your electric tool (page 13). Again making 'to order' is better than storing too much.

CURRY PASTE MIXTURE

MAKES **A**BOUT

——— 225 g (8 oz) ———

A s the ethos of this book is speed and simplicity I have used 'curry paste' as an ingredient in a great many recipes. This is good news and bad news. It's good for the ethos… it saves the time and effort of mixing and frying a number of ground spices. It could be bad news because, using the same curry paste in each recipe could cause each recipe to taste rather similar. To avoid that I have diligently used the other flavourings in each recipe to greatest effect with the result that the curry paste, whilst very important, nevertheless plays a supporting rather than a dominant role in the taste picture. You can use any brand of factory-bottled paste. Go for mild or medium, not hot. They vary a lot from manufacturer to manufacturer, in colour, texture and taste. Some pad out with salt and flour. Rather than make your own paste – a job requiring a couple of hours in the kitchen – here is a relatively easy compromise. Make up a batch of ground spices (called in India masala, over here curry powder). Note firstly the use of madras curry powder in this mixture. It contributes an extra depth of taste in the form of just enough chilli and many extra spices, without itself dominating. Note secondly the unorthodox use of packet tomato soup. Again it contributes, this time as a balancer in the savoury department. To cook with this mixture where the recipe asks for, say '1 tablespoon curry paste', simply mix 1 tablespoon of this mixture with enough water to make a paste, then add it to the recipe. You can put the dry mixture straight into the cooking, but the water minimizes the risk of it burning. It's up to you.

In volume terms the amount this recipe makes will slightly overfill a coffee mug. A tablespoon is 15 g ($^1/_2$ oz) and the average requirement in my recipes is 1 or 2 tablespoons. So this batch is enough for at least 10 curries. Store the mixture dry, as with any ground spice, in the dark in an air-tight container. Use within 6 months of making.

Measure each spice into a large mixing bowl. Mix well and put into a lidded container.

INGREDIENTS

UTENSILS
mixing bowl
PREPARATION TIME
less than 5 minutes
COOKING TIME
nil

$4^1/_2$ tablespoons ground
  coriander
3 tablespoons garlic powder
2 tablespoons paprika
2 tablespoons ground cumin
4 teaspoons madras curry
  powder
4 teaspoons packet tomato
  soup
2 teaspoons turmeric

GARAM MASALA

MAKES ABOUT

—————— 100 g (4 oz) ——————

This is a mixture of aromatic spices used to enhance certain curries. You can buy factory-ground garam masala but for an unbeatable flavour why not do the ultimate in roast and grind. Although it really does not take much effort or time to make, it is the type of job I like to do when I am not pressed for time. In volume terms 100 g (4 oz) is about half a coffee mugful. Spoon or piece measures, whilst creating variations batch to batch, will suffice. In any case you may wish to vary/add/subtract ingredients to suit your own palate when you make subsequent batches. As most recipes use 2 teaspoons or 1 tablespoon garam masala (roughly 10 g/^{1}/$_4$ oz and 15 g/^{1}/$_2$ oz respectively) 100 g (4 oz) will last for about 10 recipes. Store as for any ground spice. Use within 6 months of grinding.

Heat the dry karahi or wok (without oil or water). When hot add the coriander seeds and dry 'stir-fry'. About 30 seconds later add all the other whole spices and dry 'stir-fry' for a further minute. Let it all cool. Then grind it in your electric coffee grinder or spice mill to as fine a powder as it will give you. Stir in the ground cinnamon and cloves and store until required.

INGREDIENTS

UTENSILS
large karahi or wok
PREPARATION TIME
2 minutes
COOKING TIME
3 minutes

3^1/$_2$ tablespoons coriander
    seeds
1^1/$_2$ tablespoons white cumin
    seeds
1 tablespoon fennel seeds
10 green cardamoms
1 blade mace
3–4 bay leaves
2 teaspoons ground cinnamon
1 teaspoon ground cloves

ANY-TIME SNACKS AND TITBITS

Food vendors are a colourful part of the Indian street scene. Their stalls, often mobile, are piled high with delectable food of all kinds. They are surrounded by customers: Indians are great grazers. Little wonder – their snacks are stupendous, and there is a vast repertoire to choose from.

Of all the chapters, this was the hardest one to narrow down to just eleven choices. In the end I opted for two which are well-established favourites at the restaurant – Onion Fritters (or bhajia) and, that invention of the Raj, Mulligatawny Soup. The remaining nine recipes may not be as well known, but they are outstanding, tempting and delicious. Two are soups, four are cold, and the remaining three are quick hot dishes.

You'll notice that I have refrained from calling these dishes starters. But if you wish, and have the time, they all are absolutely perfect starters to any curry meal.

VEGETABLE CURRY BAP

SERVES

—— 4 ——

INGREDIENTS

UTENSILS
small saucepan, wok or karahi
PREPARATION TIME
3 minutes
COOKING TIME
10 minutes

1 tablespoon sunflower oil
¹/₂ teaspoon white cumin seeds
¹/₂ teaspoon black mustard seeds
1 tablespoon curry paste
2–3 tablespoons finely chopped onion
200 g (7 oz) tin baked beans
100 g (4 oz) frozen mixed vegetables
1 tablespoon tomato ketchup
¹/₂ teaspoon Worcestershire sauce
¹/₂ teaspoon garam masala
Salt to taste
4 crisp fresh bread rolls, white or brown, or baps

This is street food from the real India where it is called pao bhajee. It is a vegetable curry served hot or cold in a bread roll or bap. A super snack at any time.

Heat the oil and fry the seeds for 10 seconds. Add the curry paste and onions and stir-fry for 5 minutes or so. Add the baked beans, mixed vegetables, ketchup, Worcestershire sauce and garam masala and stir to the sizzle. Salt to taste. Serve hot or cold in or out of the rolls.

ONION FRITTERS

MAKES

—— 8 ——

Better known by their Indian name, pakoras or bhajia, and even better still by their misnomer bhajee, these fritters are, without doubt, one of the favourite Indian snacks over here. They are really easy to make at home and are astoundingly much cheaper too. And there is nothing like them, freshly cooked. They do, however, keep chilled and they freeze too (after cooking). Two things are essential. One is gram flour (see page 18) – nothing else will do. The other is a deep-fryer. You make a batter with the former whilst the latter heats up. Other than that, it is all simplicity itself, the results being an exquisitely tasty snack at any time.

———

Put the oil in your deep-fryer or saucepan (see page 14) and start heating up to 190°C (375°F) (chip-frying temperature). Whilst the oil is heating up, put the flour, seeds, ketchup, salt, paste and coconut into a large mixing bowl and add just enough water to achieve a thickish paste which just drops off the spoon. Chop the spring onions (green and white parts) and coriander leaves, and chillies (if using) and mix them well into the paste, and leave the mixture to stand for about 5 minutes. By now the oil should be hot enough. Test by putting a tiny piece of batter into the oil. It should sink, then rise up almost at once and float. Using 2 tablespoons, scoop about one-eighth of the mixture from the bowl with 1 spoon. Holding it just above the oil, carefully scrape the mixture off with the other spoon so that it slips into the oil. It will sink, then float. Repeat with 7 more spoonfuls. Deep-fry for 8–10 minutes, keeping your eye on them, and turning the bhajias once or twice. Remove from the oil, shaking off excess oil and resting them on kitchen paper. Sprinkle garam masala over them. Serve piping hot, with lemon wedges and chutneys or allow to cool and refrigerate or freeze.

INGREDIENTS

UTENSILS
deep-fryer or large saucepan, large mixing bowl
PREPARATION TIME
12 minutes
COOKING TIME
10 minutes

Vegetable or corn oil for deep-frying
100 g (4 oz) gram flour
2 teaspoons white cumin seeds
1 tablespoon tomato ketchup
1 teaspoon salt
1 tablespoon curry paste
1 tablespoon desiccated coconut
6–8 spring onions
20–25 fresh coriander leaves
1–2 fresh green chillies (optional), de-stalked
Garam masala for sprinkling
Lemon wedges and chutneys to serve

BUTTER PRAWNS

S E R V E S

—— 4 ——

UTENSILS
karahi, wok or frying-pan
PREPARATION TIME
3 minutes
COOKING TIME
5–12 minutes

2–3 tablespoons butter
1 teaspoon white cumin seeds
$^1/_2$ teaspoon turmeric
2 cloves garlic, chopped
100 g (4 oz) onion, chopped
300 g (11 oz) uncooked
    peeled prawns (any size)
2 tablespoons natural Greek
    yoghurt
1 teaspoon garam masala
1 tablespoon chopped fresh
    coriander leaves
Salt to taste
Snipped chives to garnish
Lemon or lime wedges to
    serve

Fresh peeled prawns of any size are better than frozen prawns because they yield less water content when fried. The butter coupled with the spices gives a gorgeous caramelized taste and a beautiful natural, reddy pink colour. You could serve the prawns with fresh Indian or crusty French bread or a salad.

Using your karahi, wok or frying-pan, heat the butter. As soon as it is nearly melted fry the seeds for 10 seconds. Add the turmeric and garlic and stir-fry for 30 seconds. Add the onion and prawns, lower the heat and stir-fry at a gentle sizzle until the prawns are cooked. This will depend on the thickness of the prawns, the smaller the quicker, obviously. To check, cut a prawn in half. It should be an even whitish colour right through (no sign of 'grey'). At that point add the yoghurt, garam masala, fresh coriander and salt to taste, and stir-fry for a further minute until everything is well incorporated. Serve the prawns on their own, garnished with the chives and with lemon or lime wedges.

Opposite: BUTTER PRAWNS, WITH PESHWARI NAAN *(page 109)*

CURRIED SCRAMBLED EGG

S E R V E S

—— 4 ——

I adore scrambled eggs and so do Indians. They enjoy it with spices at any time of day, including breakfast. If that's one meal too far for you, brunch might be acceptable! Serve it hot with fresh, crunchy French bread or toast dripping with butter, or cold as a sandwich filler.

Heat the butter in a small non-stick saucepan. Fry the seeds for 10 seconds. Add the turmeric and garlic and stir-fry for a further 30 seconds. Add the spring onion, coriander and chilli (if using) and stir-fry for 2–3 minutes. Break the eggs into a small bowl and whisk with a fork to mix the yolk and white. Add to the saucepan and stir until the egg sets (but doesn't go too dry). Sprinkle with salt and garam masala and serve.

INGREDIENTS

UTENSILS
small non-stick saucepan
PREPARATION TIME
3 minutes
COOKING TIME
6–7 minutes

2 tablespoons butter
$^1/_2$ teaspoon white cumin seeds
$^1/_4$ teaspoon turmeric
1 clove garlic, finely chopped
2–3 spring onions, chopped
1 tablespoon chopped fresh coriander leaves
1 fresh red chilli (optional), chopped
4 large eggs
Salt to taste
Garam masala to taste

Opposite: CHICKEN TIKKA *(page 52),* WITH PULLAO RICE *(page 112)*

UTENSILS
mixing bowl
PREPARATION TIME
10 minutes
COOKING TIME
nil

8–10 heaped tablespoons
unsweetened rice crispies
2–3 cooked popadoms,
broken up
50 g (2 oz) sev (optional)
3–4 spring onions, finely
chopped
1 tablespoon chopped fresh
coriander leaves
1–2 fresh red chillies
(optional)
¹/₃ teaspoon lovage seeds
¹/₂ teaspoon roasted white
cumin seeds
¹/₃ teaspoon roasted coriander
seeds
¹/₂ teaspoon mango powder
¹/₃ teaspoon salt
4 tablespoons cooked cold
potatoes, peeled and in
small cubes
4–6 tablespoons natural
yoghurt
¹/₃ teaspoon garam masala
1 tablespoon vinegar (any
type)
2 tablespoons tomato ketchup
1 tablespoon tomato purée
1 teaspoon paprika
1 teaspoon chilli powder
(optional)
1 teaspoon tamarind powder
1 tablespoon brown sauce

CRISPY COLD SNACK

S E R V E S

—— 4 as a snack or starter ——

This is a snack from India called bhel puri. There are a few bhel puri restaurants in Britain, and very popular they are too. Otherwise bhel puri is virtually unknown. In fact it is Bombay's absolutely favourite street snack and it's worth getting to know. You'll love it. It's a mixture of crispy rice (I'm taking the bold step of using unsweetened rice crispies – and yes it works) with potato, crunched up crisp popadoms (it saves making the more usual crisp puris) and sev (a packet squiggly snack in the Bombay-mix family). The latter can be omitted if unavailable. This mixture is served with 3 chutneys which brings it all to life.

Put the rice crispies, popadoms and sev (if using) into the mixing bowl with the spring onion, coriander leaves, chillies (if you like), seeds, mango powder and salt. Mix well and add the potato, and gently mix it in. Put the mixture aside while you make the 3 simple sauces.

For the yoghurt sauce, simply add the garam masala to the yoghurt, mix and chill.

For the red sauce, mix the vinegar, tomato ketchup and purée, paprika and chilli powder (if using) to achieve the same consistency as the yoghurt.

For the brown sauce, mix the tamarind powder with the brown sauce and enough water to achieve the same consistency. To serve (for 4) put the crisp mixture into 4 serving bowls. Put each of the 3 sauces into its own serving bowl. Allow each diner to put what they want of each sauce on to their crisp mixture, mix well and eat.

KASHMIRI MUSHROOM AND FENNEL

S E R V E S

—— 4 as a starter ——

High up in the mountains lies Kashmir, a favourite haunt of the emperors. The food there is flavoured with aromatic spices. Here I use fennel bulb and seeds and, with so many new mushroom types widely available, you can have fun with a mixture. Fresh wild mushrooms, if available, will add class to your dish. In the springtime you might be lucky enough to obtain golden spicy-tasting chanterelles or morels. This dish can be served hot. I actually prefer it cold, the flavours seem to come through better when it is cold.

Wash and peel the mushrooms, then pat them dry in kitchen paper. Heat the oil in your karahi, wok or frying-pan. Stir-fry the seeds and cardamoms for 10 seconds. Add the ginger and stir-fry for 10 more seconds. Next add the spring onions and the chopped fennel and stir-fry for about 5 minutes. You will need a splash or two of water to keep things mobile. Meanwhile slice the mushrooms, then add them to the pan. After a couple more minutes add the walnut, mint, garam masala and salt to taste. Sizzle on for a minute or so more. Serve on its own, hot or cold.

INGREDIENTS

UTENSILS
karahi, wok or frying-pan
PREPARATION TIME
5 minutes
COOKING TIME
10 minutes

120–150 g (4¹/₂–5 oz)
mushrooms (any type)
2 tablespoons pistachio or
walnut oil
³/₄ teaspoon fennel seeds
¹/₄ teaspoon black cumin seeds
3–4 green cardamoms,
crushed
2.5 cm (1 inch) piece fresh
ginger, thinly sliced into
strips
3–4 spring onions, chopped
1 fennel bulb, chopped into
small pieces
1 tablespoon chopped walnuts
6–8 fresh mint leaves,
chopped
Garam masala to taste
Salt to taste

CUMIN-FLAVOURED LIVER STIR-FRY

S E R V E S

—— 4 as a starter ——

It's truly great, this recipe. Liver makes an easy stir-fry subject. The red accompaniment enhances the liver's natural colours and the cumin (and I've used both black and white) enhances its flavour. You can use bought tandoori paste if you are short of time. Serve hot on its own or perhaps with fresh bread.

Heat the ghee in your karahi, wok or frying-pan. Fry all the seeds for 10 seconds. Add the garlic and stir-fry for 30 seconds. Add the onion and the paste and stir-fry for a couple of minutes more. Then add the liver, and stir-fry from time to time. Cook for 5 minutes. Add the tomato purée, pepper, chilli (if using) and basil leaves and carry on stir-frying until the liver is fully cooked but is still very succulent (about 5 more minutes should do it). Cut a piece in half – it should not be red in the centre. Add the garam masala and salt to taste. Stir well. Allow the liver to rest for a couple of minutes for the flavours to blend and the liver to soften. Garnish with the chives.

INGREDIENTS

UTENSILS
karahi, wok or frying-pan
PREPARATION TIME
5 minutes
COOKING TIME
15 minutes

2 tablespoons ghee
2 teaspoons sesame seeds
1 teaspoon white cumin seeds
$^1/_8$ teaspoon black cumin seeds
2 cloves garlic, chopped
50 g (2 oz) onion, finely
   chopped
2 teaspoons Tandoori Paste
   (see page 44)
300 g to 350 g (11–12 oz)
   lambs' liver, cut into
   2.5 cm (1 inch) pieces
1 tablespoon tomato purée
2 tablespoons finely chopped
   red pepper
1–2 fresh red chilli, finely
   chopped (optional)
4–6 fresh basil leaves,
   chopped
1 teaspoon garam masala
Salt to taste
Snipped chives to garnish

POTATOES IN A PICKLY SAUCE

SERVES

—— 4 as part of a starter ——

This is one of my favourites. I often serve it as part of a starter at dinner parties. It's quick (virtually instant in fact), tasty and popular. Served cold it can be prepared well in advance. It improves with marination, kept in the fridge.

Chop the large bits of pickled aubergine into small pieces. Strain the tinned potatoes, keeping the liquid for soup or stock. Put them in the mixing bowl. Add the curry paste, the chopped pickle, leaves, chilli (if liked) and yoghurt and gently stir around to mix well. Salt to taste. Chill and serve.

INGREDIENTS

UTENSILS
mixing bowl
PREPARATION TIME
3 minutes
COOKING TIME
nil

---

4 tablespoons aubergine (brinjal) pickle
400 g (14 oz) tin peeled baby potatoes
1 teaspoon curry paste
1 tablespoon chopped fresh coriander leaves
1 fresh red chilli, chopped (optional)
1 tablespoon natural Greek yoghurt
Salt to taste

MULLIGATAWNY SOUP

S E R V E S

—— 4 ——

UTENSILS
large lidded saucepan
PREPARATION TIME
2–3 minutes
COOKING TIME
about 25 minutes

2 tablespoons vegetable oil
1 teaspoon mustard seeds
1 teaspoon sesame seeds
$^1/_2$ teaspoon white cumin
  seeds
$^1/_3$ teaspoon lovage seeds
$^1/_2$ teaspoon turmeric
2 cloves garlic, chopped
1 large onion, coarsely
  chopped
2 tablespoons curry paste
750 ml ($1^1/_4$ pints) stock or
  water
3–4 bay leaves
1 cup vegetable and/or meat
  'left-overs'
Salt to taste
Squeeze of lemon (optional)

If your fridge is like mine, it is home to a bowl of this and a plate of that, a dish of something else – all worthy left-overs from previous meals – all with plenty of goodness left in them. What to do with these items? Well here's one of my stock answers: Mulligatawny Soup, that stalwart of the Raj. Obviously what each version contains will depend on what left-overs are in the fridge. You need about 1 cupful of left-overs. If you have more, make a larger mulligatawny and freeze spares. Thus not only is this a wonderfully economical non-wasting recipe, the result is really souperb [sic].

Heat the oil in a large saucepan. Fry the seeds for about 10 seconds. Add the turmeric and garlic and stir-fry for 30 seconds more. Add the onion and the curry paste and stir-fry for about 3 minutes. Add the stock or water, and the bay leaves and bring to the simmer. Add the left-overs and simmer for at least 10 minutes, to ensure they are well softened. Salt to taste. A squeeze of lemon juice is a nice option.

CURRIED CRAB CHOWDER

S E R V E S

—— 4 ——

Using a small tin of crab, this becomes a very tasty curried soup. It is rich, though, so a little goes a long way. Delicious with crusty French bread or ciabatta.

Heat the butter in the large saucepan. Fry the seeds for 10 seconds then add the paste, onion, celery, red pepper and chilli and stir-fry for about 5 minutes. Add the crab, bay leaves and the water or stock. Bring to the simmer. Add enough milk to the cornflour to make a creamy paste. Then add to the saucepan with the rest of the milk. Simmer for a further 5 minutes. Salt to taste. Place into serving bowls, curling on some cream and garnishing with chives.

INGREDIENTS

UTENSILS
large lidded saucepan
PREPARATION TIME
3 minutes
COOKING TIME
12 minutes

2 tablespoons butter

1 teaspoon fennel seeds

1 teaspoon Tandoori Paste
(see page 44)

50 g (2 oz) onion, finely
chopped

50 g (2 oz) celery, finely
chopped

1 tablespoon finely chopped
red pepper

1 tablespoon finely chopped
fresh green chillies

100 g (4 oz) tinned white
crabmeat

2 bay leaves

450 ml (15 fl oz) water or
stock

120 ml (4 fl oz) milk

1 tablespoon cornflour

Salt to taste

50 ml (2 fl oz) single cream

Snipped chives to garnish

HERBAL RASAM SOUP

SERVES

—— 4 ——

UTENSILS
large lidded saucepan
PREPARATION TIME
3 minutes
COOKING TIME
25–30 minutes

2 tablespoons sesame oil
1 teaspoon mustard seeds
1 teaspoon sesame seeds
$^1/_2$ teaspoon lovage seeds
$^1/_2$ teaspoon turmeric
$^1/_2$ teaspoon mango powder
2–3 cloves garlic, sliced
1–2 fresh red chillies
  (optional), chopped
4–6 spring onions, chopped
900 ml (1$^1/_2$ pints) water or
  stock
1 tablespoon vinegar (any
  type)
1 tablespoon red lentils
2 tablespoons frozen peas
2 tablespoons chopped fresh
  coriander leaves
1 tablespoon chopped fresh
  basil leaves
Salt to taste
Sugar to taste
Snipped chives to garnish

Down in South India they are never far away from a rasam. It's a sort of national dish – a light consommé served hot, and spiked with hot spices. A good friend of mine, who lives in Bangalore, actually keeps a Wedgwood Florentine teapot complete with cups and saucers, just for the purpose of serving rasam, virtually at any time of day. This version, wallowing in green herbs, is fresh and refreshing on its own or to start the meal. It can be made a day or two in advance and can be frozen.

Heat the oil. Fry the seeds for 10 seconds. Add the turmeric, mango powder, garlic, chilli (if using), and onion and stir-fry for about 3 minutes. Add the water or stock, vinegar, lentils and peas. Simmer for about 20 minutes. Add the fresh leaves, salt and sugar to taste. Simmer for 5–10 minutes more. At this point, if preferred, you can strain the soup and discard the solids. Put into serving bowls (or Florentine cups) garnished with the chives.

TIKKA AND TANDOORI

If anything has put Indian food on the Western map, it is tandoori and tikka cooking. The process, originally from north Pakistan, is charcoal cooking using a clay oven called the tandoor. Tikka literally means 'a little piece', so chicken tikka is a tandoori-cooked piece of chicken. Also meat and chicken are usually marinated for up to 60 hours. Especially for this chapter, I have developed recipes which need no marinade, although if you plan ahead and allow the time, marination will improve flavours. Two recipes need the oven (the tandoori boneless chicken, and potato) and 45 minutes cooking time. The king prawn, meat and chicken tikkas need the grill and take between 10 and 20 minutes to cook. The Sheek Kebabs need a tool to grind the meat down, then they are grilled, so though they could be accused of being labour-intensive, they are well worth the minor effort involved. The mushrooms only take 10 minutes to make, and there are two cold dishes – the prawn cocktail and the avocado crab. Any of these recipes can work as an any-time snack or light meal or, if you have enough time, as a starter.

*H*OME-MADE
QUICK TANDOORI PASTE

M A K E S

—— about 350 g (12 oz) ——

Use factory-made, bottled tandoori paste by all means if you have no qualms about red food colouring. If you want a chemical-free substitute without the long process of cooking it, here is my near-enough alternative, using bottled curry paste. It requires no cooking and will last indefinitely.

Simply mix all the ingredients together and put it into clean, dry jars. A heaped teaspoon of paste is an average amount for one portion. Use by the spoonful as directed in the recipes.

INGREDIENTS

UTENSILS
mixing bowl, lidded jars
PREPARATION TIME
5 minutes
COOKING TIME
nil

200 g (7 oz) bottled mild or medium curry paste

15 g roasted coriander seeds, ground

1 tablespoon garam masala

3 teaspoons paprika

2 teaspoons roasted cumin seeds, ground

1 teaspoon mango powder

1–3 teaspoons chilli powder

4 tablespoons vinegar from bottled beetroot

4 teaspoons granulated white sugar

1 tablespoon bottled vinegared mint

2 teaspoons salt

SUPER-FAST TANDOORI MARINADE

M A K E S

—— about 400 g (14 oz) ——

As this is needed for several recipes, it is easier to give it separately rather than to keep repeating it. Don't reduce the garlic content unless you really must. It is one of the tasty secrets of the marinade. A good tip for tandoori/tikka fans is to make up a full batch of this marinade for spontaneous use of all or part of it in the relevant recipes in this chapter. If you use new fresh yoghurt, the marinade can be kept in the fridge, stored in yoghurt pots, right up to the yoghurt's use-by date, which should be several days.

———

Put all the ingredients, except the milk, into the blender or food processor. Pulse to a purée using enough milk to make it easily pourable but not thin. Store in yoghurt pots in the fridge and use as required.

INGREDIENTS

UTENSILS
blender or food processor
PREPARATION TIME
5 minutes
COOKING TIME
nil

*150 g (5 oz) natural Greek
  yoghurt*
4 cloves garlic
*2.5 cm (1 inch) piece fresh
  ginger*
1 tablespoon sesame oil
*1 tablespoon chopped red
  pepper*
*1–2 fresh red chillies
  (optional), chopped*
2 tablespoons tomato purée
*1 tablespoon chopped fresh
  coriander leaves*
*1 tablespoon chopped fresh
  mint leaves*
1 teaspoon salt
*About 100 ml (3¹/₂ fl oz)
  milk*

SHEEK KEBABS

S E R V E S

—— 4 ——

The sheek kebab is rightly one of the restaurant favourites. There are a number of ways of making them, but this one is fool-proof and delicious. The secret is to avoid butcher's mince and using best-quality chunks of meat and the scimitar blade of the food processor, produce your own ground mixture, incorporating garlic, ginger, spices and herbs. This way you achieve a gristle-free, glutinous, dry mixture which can be moulded into shapes or optionally on skewers. The processor makes it easy, and the shaping and cooking is really quite quick. Use the waiting time to sample some cooking wine or make another dish! Kebabs can be made in advance and frozen uncooked or cooked. Serve them with salad and lemon wedges.

First, decide whether you will grill the kebabs or use the oven. Pre-heat which one you choose – the oven to 190°C/375°F/Gas 5, or the grill to medium heat.

Chop the meat into small strips or cubes (removing all fat and gristle etc.) suitable for the food processor. Put a sensible amount of meat into the processor bowl along with a proportional amount of the other ingredients. Pulse until you have an even, smooth mixture relatively lump-free. Put this into a mixing bowl and do another batch in the processor until everything is ground. Put it into the bowl too and give everything a thorough mix with your fingers to ensure all the ingredients are equally distributed. Divide the mixture into 4, shaping into rounds or sausages and optionally using skewers. Place them on to a rack above a foil-lined tray and into the oven or under the grill at the midway position. Cook for about 6 minutes, then turn them over. Cook for about 6 more minutes. Serve immediately.

INGREDIENTS

UTENSILS
food processor, mixing bowl, oven or grill rack, foil-lined tray
PREPARATION TIME
6–8 minutes
COOKING TIME
12 minutes

650 g (1 lb 6 oz) lean steak

4 cloves garlic, chopped

5 cm (2 inch) piece fresh ginger, chopped

2 teaspoons roasted cumin seeds

1 teaspoon roasted coriander seeds

1 tablespoon curry paste or Tandoori Paste (see page 44)

1 teaspoon garam masala

1 teaspoon salt

2 tablespoons chopped fresh coriander leaves

1 tablespoon chopped fresh basil leaves

4 spring onions (green parts only), chopped

TANDOORI PRAWN COCKTAIL

SERVES
—— 4 ——

Once the height of sophistication, the prawn cocktail has rather fallen from grace. Yet, it is a clever presentation. Shredded lettuce in a stemmed glass with pink mayonnaise and cooked prawns. Here, in a simple and very effective conversion, the mayonnaise is replaced with Tandoori Marinade. If you haven't any marinade already made in the fridge, this cocktail still does not take long to prepare.

Shred the lettuce and the spring onions and mix with the fresh coriander and pinch of garam masala. Put enough of this mixture loosely into each glass, to about the half-way mark. Mix the prawns and the marinade together and fill the glass to the brim with it. Sprinkle a little paprika or chilli and a few coriander leaves on top. Top with a thin lime wedge or two. Keep in the fridge until required.

INGREDIENTS

UTENSILS
4 stemmed glasses
PREPARATION TIME
4 minutes
COOKING TIME
nil

3–4 lettuce leaves
2–3 spring onions
1 tablespoon fresh coriander leaves, chopped
Pinch of garam masala
250 g (9 oz) cooked prawns
200 g (7 oz) Tandoori Marinade (see page 45)

TO SERVE
Paprika or chilli powder
A few whole coriander leaves
Some thin lime wedges

TANDOORI
BONELESS CHICKEN

SERVES
—— 4 ——

INGREDIENTS

UTENSILS
mixing bowl, oven tray and rack
PREPARATION TIME
10 minutes
MARINATION TIME
nil–60 hours
COOKING TIME
45 minutes

900 g–1.25 kg (2 lb–2¹/₂ lb) boneless chicken, skinned
Juice of 1 lemon
Salt
400 g (14 oz) Tandoori Marinade (see page 45)
TO SERVE
Salad leaves
Garam masala
Snipped chive leaves
Chilli powder (optional)
Lemon or lime wedges

Yes, you can buy boneless chicken all trussed up and ready to cook. It's a fiddly job if you want to bone it yourself, so don't. You will have to skin it but that's effortless. The marinade is fast to make and if you want a quick result coat the chicken and oven-bake it immediately. If you have planned for this dish a day or two ahead, put the chicken into the marinade in a non-metallic mixing bowl. Cover and refrigerate for up to 60 hours for a fresh chicken and 24 for one which has been frozen and thawed first. You can freeze this dish after cooking, but only if it was a fresh chicken to start with. Serve with raita and naan bread.

If you intend to cook the chicken without marinating first, pre-heat the oven to 190°C/375°F/Gas 5 and line an oven tray with foil putting the rack over it.

Wash and dry the skinless chicken inside and out. Score shallow gashes on the flesh with a sharp knife. Massage the flesh with the lemon juice and lightly sprinkle with salt. Make the marinade (see page 45). Put the chicken into the bowl and massage the marinade into the flesh. If marinating, cover the bowl and refrigerate for 24–60 hours (see introduction).

To cook, remove the chicken from the bowl and fold it back into a 'chicken-shape'. Place it on the rack upside-down and place it into the pre-heated oven. Retain any excess marinade in the bowl. Cook the chicken for 20 minutes. Remove it from the oven, drain off cooking liquid for stock and turn the chicken the right way up. Pour all the remaining marinade on to it. Return to the oven for a further 20 minutes. Inspect and check that it is cooked by poking a skewer into the thickest flesh. If clear liquid runs out, baste it with cooking liquid and give it a final 5 minutes cooking. If the juices are not clear, baste and cook until it is ready. Prior to serving, carve it into slices. Place these on to a bed of salad leaves. Sprinkle with garam masala, chives and chilli powder. Serve with lemon or lime wedges.

TANDOORI KING PRAWNS

S E R V E S

—— 4 as a starter ——

The bigger the prawn the better for this recipe. The biggest are sometimes called tiger prawns and are as much as 100 g (4 oz) each when peeled. One is enough per person for a starter. Average king prawns are about 25 g (1 oz) each, so you'll need 4 per person. The prawns can be marinated for up to 6 hours if you have time, if not don't worry. Serve the prawns with raita and naan bread.

Pre-heat the grill to medium heat.

Wash the prawns and pat dry. Massage with the lemon juice and set aside. Make the marinade according to the recipe on page 45. Put the prawns into the marinade (they can be marinated for up to 6 hours or simply immersed in the marinade if you don't have time). Put the prawns on to a rack over a foil-lined grill pan and place the pan midway under the heat. Grill for between 4 and 6 minutes (depending on prawn thickness). Turn and cook for a further 4 or 6 minutes. Sprinkle with garam masala, optional chilli powder and garnish with fresh coriander leaves. Serve on a bed of salad with lemon or lime wedges.

INGREDIENTS

UTENSILS
foil-lined grill pan
PREPARATION TIME
5 minutes
MARINATION TIME
nil–6 hours
COOKING TIME
8–12 minutes

450 g (1 lb) uncooked king prawns, peeled
Juice of 1 lemon
200 g (7 oz) Tandoori Marinade (see page 45)

TO SERVE
Garam masala
Chilli powder (optional)
Fresh coriander leaves to garnish
Salad leaves
Lemon or lime wedges

TANDOORI BAKED POTATO

SERVES
—— 4 ——

INGREDIENTS

UTENSILS
oven tray and rack
PREPARATION TIME
5 minutes
COOKING TIME
1¼ hours

4 large baking potatoes
200 g (7 oz) Tandoori
  Marinade (see page 45)
TO SERVE
Garam masala
Chilli powder (optional)
Salt to taste

In the strongly Muslim meat-eating area of Pakistan where tandoori developed, the potato (in any case an American alien) is taken as seriously as all other vegetables i.e. it has no part in the tandoori repertoire. However, cooking foil and the oven make the tandoori baked potato a must. Double foil-wrapping prevents burning. Although the cooking time is quite long, there is no labour involved. Serve as an accompaniment to sausages or burgers – kebabs even.

Pre-heat the oven to 160°C/325°F/Gas 3.

Scrub the potatoes, but don't bother to peel them. Remove scars and 'eyes' and, using a small knife or skewer, gouge out small holes to give the marinade a greater surface area to penetrate. Make the marinade according to the recipe on page 45. Coat the potatoes generously with it, and cover each carefully with foil. Then cover each one again with a double wrap. Put the potatoes on a rack or tray into the oven and bake for about 1¼ hours. Then poke with a skewer to test there is no hard centre. (Cook further if there is.) Carefully remove the foil. Sprinkle with garam masala, optional chilli and salt to taste.

MEAT TIKKA

S E R V E S

—— 4 ——

L amb or mutton is the usual meat used for this at the restaurant. Lamb is fattier than beef and takes longer to cook. Pork, venison and veal can also be used. Leg is the best cut. Here I am using the most expensive meat – fillet steak. You can use cheaper cuts, of course, but you'll get out what you put in and there is no disguising poor quality meat in this recipe. Like steak, meat tikka should be chewy and beef is acceptable slightly rare, if you like it that way. So cooking time is minimal under the grill. Serve with salad, lemon wedges and bread.

Cut the steak into approximately 3 cm (1¼ inch) cubes, aiming to obtain 4–5 pieces per person (16–20 pieces in total). Make the marinade according to the recipe on page 45. Put the meat into it and, if you have time, marinate it for up to 60 hours (fresh meat only) and 24 hours (frozen and thawed meat). If you want quicker tikka omit the marination but baste the cubes and put them on to the 4 skewers and then a foil-lined grill pan. Place midway under the grill, pre-heated to medium heat. Cook for 6–8 minutes. Turn the skewers and carry on cooking for a further 6–8 minutes. You can turn the skewers more frequently if you wish. Your total cooking time is between 12–16 minutes and will depend on how well cooked you want the tikkas.

INGREDIENTS

UTENSILS
4 skewers, foil-lined grill pan
PREPARATION TIME
6 minutes
MARINATION TIME
nil–60 hours
COOKING TIME
12–16 minutes

550 g (1¼ lb) fillet steak
400 g (14 oz) Tandoori
Marinade (see page 45)

CHICKEN TIKKA

S E R V E S

—— 4 ——

INGREDIENTS

UTENSILS
4 skewers, foil-lined grill pan
PREPARATION TIME
6 minutes
MARINATION TIME
nil–60 hours
COOKING TIME
10–15 minutes

550 g (1¹/₄ lb) boned and
*   skinned chicken breast*
Juice of 1 lemon
400 g (14 oz) Tandoori
*   Marinade (see page 45)*
TO SERVE
Garam masala
Chilli powder
Salad leaves
Lemon wedges

Hard to believe, isn't it, that hardly anyone over here had heard of Chicken Tikka before the 1970s. Today it stands head and shoulders over all other ethnic dishes in popularity polls. It now appears in all sorts of guises as sandwich filler, mayonnaise flavouring, as pizza topping, in lasagne and, of course, as itself – the favourite starter at the curry house. Here's my instant version. Without the tandoori oven, it will not have quite the same flavour but it's good all the same and you can use it in sandwiches, mayonnaise, pizza or lasagne if you wish or simply serve it in the straight, traditional, delicious way. Accompany it with raitas, chutneys and naan bread.

Cut the chicken into pieces averaging about 3–4 cm (1¹/₄–1¹/₂ inches) aiming for 4–5 pieces per person (16 to 20 in total). Make the marinade according to the recipe on page 45. Immerse the chicken pieces. You can marinate them, covered in the fridge, for up to 60 hours (fresh chicken only) and 24 hours (frozen and thawed chicken). For 'instant' results put the pieces on to the 4 skewers and on to a foil-lined grill pan and midway under the grill, preheated to medium heat. Cook for 5 minutes, then turn the skewers and cook for 5–8 minutes more (exact time depends on chicken piece thickness). Chicken must be cooked right through. If you are not sure, cut one piece in half. It must not show any sign of 'rareness'. If it does, cook on. Prior to serving sprinkle on some garam masala and chilli powder. Serve on a salad bed with lemon wedges.

PRAWN AND MUSHROOM TIKKA STIR-FRY

SERVES

—— 4 ——

This recipe is one of my real favourites and it is really quick and easy. Peeled cooked prawns are simply stir-fried with Tandoori Marinade. If it is already made up in the fridge (and I assume it is, in the preparation time below) it is perhaps the fastest hot curry in this book. Serve with fresh crusty (or Indian) bread.

———

Heat the ghee. Stir-fry the seeds for 10 seconds. Add the garlic and stir-fry this for 30 seconds. Add the marinade and stir-fry for 3–4 minutes, during which time it will thicken and change colour. Add the pepper, chilli (if using), fresh leaves, garam masala, mushrooms and prawns. Briskly stir-fry for a further 3–4 minutes, ensuring the prawns are hot right through. Salt to taste, then garnish with snipped chives and serve with the lemon wedges.

INGREDIENTS

UTENSILS
karahi, wok or large frying-pan
PREPARATION TIME
2 minutes
COOKING TIME
10 minutes

2 tablespoons ghee
1 teaspoon white cumin seeds
1 teaspoon black mustard
  seeds
2 cloves garlic, chopped
6 tablespoons Tandoori
  Marinade (see page 45)
1 tablespoon chopped green
  pepper
1–2 red chillies (optional),
  chopped
1 tablespoon chopped fresh
  coriander leaves
2 teaspoons garam masala
100 g (4 oz) button
  mushrooms, sliced
500 g (1 lb 2 oz) cooked
  prawns
Salt to taste
Snipped chives to garnish
Lemon wedges to serve

TANDOORI AVOCADO CRAB

S E R V E S

—— 4 ——

You won't find the avocado in India – it's a Mexican native – but its sexy smoothness and the creamy softness of crab combine, with the tangy tastiness of tandoori, to make an exceptional dish. Don't let its speed and simplicity deceive you: it is a classy dish suitable for any occasion. Even if you do not have some Tandoori Marinade already in your fridge it's very fast.

Mix the crabmeat with the marinade and salt to taste. Chill if you wish. Just prior to serving, halve and de-stone the avocados. Carefully place the crab mixture into and on to the avocado. Garnish with the seeds and leaves and, for whose who can't live without, a halved de-stalked chilli.

INGREDIENTS

UTENSILS
glass dish
PREPARATION TIME
3 minutes
COOKING TIME
nil

100 g (4 oz) tinned crabmeat
About 4 tablespoons
    Tandoori Marinade (see
    page 45)
Salt to taste
2 ripe avocados

TO GARNISH
Roasted cumin seeds
Fresh coriander leaves
Half a small fresh red chilli
    (optional)

MEAT CURRIES

Contrary to popular belief, there are fewer vegetarians in India than meat eaters. And there is nothing like a good meat curry. Requiring longer cooking than poultry, fish or vegetables, meat absorbs spicy flavours, whilst exuding its own juices. The tastes and textures of really tender curried meat cannot be bettered. The problem is that you cannot achieve any of this quickly. And of all the chapters in this book, it is this one over which I agonized the most. Should I include traditional meat curries taking time to make or should I omit them altogether? Finally, I decided that a 10–15 minute initial start-up on the stove followed by 45–60 minutes casseroling in the oven was acceptable, particularly if you plan ahead (see page 11).

So here are eleven meat curries, using lamb, beef, and pork. Most are well-loved favourites with three or four lesser-known dishes. Most of these recipes are casseroled. But if you simply can't wait that long I have devised three recipes which are quick methods requiring just 18–20 minutes to cook. Do find the time to try them all. I promise you they are easy.

TRADITIONAL AROMATIC LAMB KORMA

UTENSILS
lidded casserole pot (see page 12)
PREPARATION TIME
5 minutes
COOKING TIME
55 minutes

750 g (1¹/₂ lb) lean leg of lamb, cut into 4 cm (1¹/₂ inch) cubes
150 g (5 oz) natural Greek yoghurt
10 cm (4 inch) cinnamon stick
4–5 bay leaves
1 small fresh green chilli, chopped
3 tablespoons butter ghee
2 brown cardamoms, crushed
5–6 green cardamoms, crushed
7–8 cloves
¹/₂ teaspoon fennel seeds
¹/₂ teaspoon black cumin seeds
2–3 star anise
1 teaspoon turmeric
4–5 cloves garlic, chopped
2 inch (5 cm) piece fresh ginger, chopped
225 g (8 oz) onion, chopped
4 tablespoons ground almonds
2 tablespoons shelled, unsalted pistachio nuts
20–30 strands saffron
100 ml (3¹/₂ fl oz) single cream
2 tablespoons chopped fresh coriander leaves
2–3 teaspoons garam masala
Salt to taste

SERVES

—— 4 ——

There are hundreds, maybe thousands, of ways of cooking korma in India – indeed the word korma means a method of cooking. It does not mean 'mild'. There are really hot Kashmiri kormas infested with chillies, for example. Real kormas involve dairy products and aromatics, and the result is a delicate pale-gold, buff-coloured, creamy-textured, subtle-flavoured dish. The green chilli should not be omitted. It enhances the aromatics but does not make the dish hot.

Combine the meat with the yoghurt and cinnamon, bay leaves and chilli and set aside. Pre-heat the oven to 190°C/375°F/Gas 5.

Heat the ghee in your casserole pot. Fry the cardamoms, cloves, seeds, star anise and turmeric for 20 seconds. Add the garlic and stir-fry for 30 seconds. Add the ginger and onion, lower the heat and stir-fry for about 5 more minutes. Add the yoghurted meat and continue to stir-fry for 5 more minutes. Then put the lid on the pot and place it in the oven. After 20 minutes, stir it round, adding a little water if required. Repeat 15 minutes later. This time add the ground almonds, pistachio nuts, saffron, cream, fresh coriander, garam masala and salt to taste. Cook for at least 5 more minutes (giving a total oven time of 40 minutes) or until really tender (which may be as much as 20 more minutes).

BALTI BEEF WITH CHICK PEAS AND SPINACH

S E R V E S

—— 4 ——

UTENSILS
balti pan, large karahi or wok
PREPARATION TIME
10 minutes
COOKING TIME
18 minutes maximum

B alti curries originate from the northernmost part of Pakistan. The balti is the name of the two-handled cooking pot, elsewhere called the karahi. The curry is stir-fried and served in the same pot. You can, of course, use a wok. Balti's distinction, apart from its rapid cooking method – stir-frying – is that it is fresh and aromatic, and wonderfully herby. For that reason, I prefer to recommend that it is eaten immediately rather than being chilled or frozen. The other wonderful thing about balti is that you can combine anything with anything. Here it is beef with chick peas and spinach. Of course you can use anything you happen to have to hand. To speed up the cooking process, use thinly sliced strips of beaten minute steak. It does not take long to make, and can be eaten with chapati, or naan (traditionally without cutlery!) or Western bread accompanied by raita and chutneys.

Beat the minute steak a little (to flatten and tenderize it) and cut into strips. Open the chick-pea tin and strain, keeping the liquid for later. Heat the oil and fry the seeds for 10 seconds. Add the garlic and stir-fry for 30 seconds more. Add the ginger and the spring onions and stir-fry for 3–4 more minutes. Add the curry paste, garam masala and tomato purée and a spoonful or two of chick pea liquid and stir-fry for 3 more minutes. Add the beef strips and briskly stir-fry the entire mixture for 5 more minutes. Add the spinach, chopped herbs, coconut, mango chutney, ketchup, tomatoes, chick peas, and enough chick pea liquid to keep things mobile. Continue stir-frying until the spinach is nice and soft and the meat tender – about 5 minutes should be ample. Salt to taste. Serve at once with a sprinkling of garam masala and coriander leaves.

500 g (1 lb 2 oz) minute steak
200 g (7 oz) tinned chick peas and their liquid
3 tablespoons sunflower oil
1 teaspoon white cumin seeds
³/₄ teaspoon fennel seeds
³/₄ teaspoon sesame seeds
¹/₃ teaspoon wild onion seeds
¹/₂ teaspoon coriander seeds
3–5 cloves garlic, finely chopped
5 cm (2 inch) piece fresh ginger, finely chopped
4–5 spring onions, chopped
1 teaspoon curry paste
2 tablespoons garam masala
1 tablespoon tomato purée
6–8 fresh spinach leaves, chopped
2 tablespoons chopped fresh coriander leaves
1 tablespoon chopped fresh mint leaves
2 tablespoons coconut milk powder
1 tablespoon chopped mango chutney
1 tablespoon tomato ketchup
2–3 tinned plum tomatoes, chopped
Salt to taste
Garam masala to garnish
Whole fresh coriander or mint leaves to garnish

GRILLED SPICY LAMB CHOPS

SERVES

— 4 —

UTENSILS
mixing bowl, foil-lined oven tray and rack
MARINATION TIME
nil–24 hours
PREPARATION TIME
4 minutes
COOKING TIME
about 30 minutes

150 g (5 oz) natural Greek yoghurt
1 tablespoon curry paste
1 tablespoon tomato purée
2 teaspoons paprika
2 teaspoons sugar
1 teaspoon garam masala
¹/₂ teaspoon salt
8 lamb chops, about 175 g (6 oz) each

The lamb chop is not a cut of meat to be found in the subcontinent, nor at the local curry house – at least not at many. Yet lamb chop is a splendid way of presenting meat. It can be rather fatty, though, and I find the oven more effective (and less messy) than the grill. Time in the oven depends on the thickness of the chop, and the degree of char you want, hence the time variation. Personally I prefer really well-done, crispy, slightly burnt chops. Note how the spicy coating is added progressively during the cooking (this is to minimize the risk of it burning).

Pre-heat the oven to 190°C/375°F/Gas 5.

Combine all the ingredients bar the chops in the mixing bowl to make the coating sauce, adding just enough water to make it drop easily off a spoon. Massage it well into the chops (optionally they can now be kept in the fridge for up to 24 hours). Shake or scrape into the bowl as much marinade as you can. Put the chops on to the rack on a tray and into the oven. After 10 minutes turn them over. After 10 more minutes, spoon about half the remaining coating sauce over them. After 10 more minutes, turn the chops and spoon the rest of the sauce over them. Don't forget to vary cooking time up or down according to taste and chop size.

PAN-FRIED PASANDA

S E R V E S

—— 4 ——

Traditionally pasanda is beaten meat, usually mutton or goat, very slowly cooked in a spicy gravy. Here I'm breaking with tradition and using minute steak and adding cream and red wine to the gravy. Not only does this make pan-frying a sensible option, it makes for the quickest meat curry in this book, and a French-style sauce which gives the dish a *'je-ne-sais-quoi'* quality. I do know what to do with any excess wine though… drink it while you're slaving at the stove!

Beat out the steaks to about 4 mm (¹/₄ in) thickness and cut them into manageable strips. Heat the ghee in the frying-pan. Fry the peppercorns, seeds and cardamoms for about 10 seconds. Add the garlic and stir-fry it for about 30 seconds. Add the curry paste and spring onion and continue stir-frying for at least 5 minutes. Add the steaks to the pan and fry them for a couple of minutes, turning once or twice to brown them. Add the cream, garam masala and the fresh leaves and stir frequently until the meat is nearly tender. Five minutes should do, but taste to test. When it is done, add the wine and salt to taste. Simmer for the 2–3 minutes needed to tenderize the meat sufficiently, then serve.

INGREDIENTS

UTENSILS
large frying-pan
PREPARATION TIME
3 minutes
COOKING TIME
18 minutes

750 g (1¹/₂ lb) minute steaks
2 tablespoons ghee
¹/₂–1 teaspoon black
   peppercorns
1 teaspoon fennel seeds
¹/₂ teaspoon white cumin
   seeds
¹/₃ teaspoon lovage seeds
4–5 green cardamoms
4 cloves garlic, finely chopped
1 tablespoon Tandoori Paste
   (see page 44) or curry paste
4 to 6 spring onions,
   shredded
100 ml (3¹/₂ fl oz) single
   cream
1–2 teaspoons garam masala
1 tablespoon chopped fresh
   basil and/or mint leaves
65 ml (2¹/₂ fl oz) red wine
Salt to taste

KARAHI STIR-FRIED MEAT
WITH GREEN HERBS

UTENSILS
large karahi or wok
PREPARATION TIME
12 minutes
COOKING TIME
20 minutes

S E R V E S

—— 4 ——

650 g (1 lb 6 oz) lean veal
escalope
3 tablespoons sunflower oil
1 teaspoon white cumin seeds
1 teaspoon black mustard
seeds
$^1/_2$ teaspoon green peppercorns
in brine
2 cloves garlic, chopped
2.5 cm (1 inch) piece root
ginger, chopped
1 tablespoon curry paste
4–6 spring onions, chopped
$^1/_2$ red pepper, cut into small
diamonds
1–2 fresh green chillies,
chopped
3–4 spinach leaves, chopped
2–3 tablespoons chopped
celery
12 cherry tomatoes, halved
1 tablespoon tomato ketchup
6–8 button mushrooms,
quartered
1 tablespoon chopped fresh
coriander leaves
1 tablespoon chopped fresh
basil leaves
1 tablespoon chopped fresh
mint leaves
2 teaspoons garam masala
2 tablespoons coconut milk
powder
Salt to taste

This is a 20-minute meat stir-fry. It's quick time for meat and it is only possible if we cut the meat into smaller than usual cubes. I recommend veal for this – escalope is easy enough to cut into 1.5 cm ($^5/_8$ inch) cubes, and it cooks relatively quickly. The karahi is, of course, the traditional Indian cooking pot, and this dish could be served in it too, diners transferring their required portion to smaller karahis or plates. It will cook just as well in a wok, but it will stick in a frying-pan or saucepan. Serve with French or Indian bread, or rice.

Cut the veal into approximately 1.5 cm ($^5/_8$ inch) cubes. Heat the oil in the karahi or wok. Fry the seeds and peppercorns for 10 seconds. Add the garlic and ginger and stir-fry for about a minute. Add the curry paste and spring onion and stir-fry for 3–4 more minutes. Add the veal and stir-fry it for a minute to 'seal' it. Add the red pepper, chilli, spinach and celery and a few tablespoons of water – just enough to 'release' everything. Continue to stir-fry for about 5 more minutes. Add the tomatoes, tomato ketchup, mushrooms, leaves and garam masala, and carry on stir-frying until the meat is as tender as you want it. This will be a further 10 minutes minimum. Stir in the coconut and salt to taste.

HOT HOTTER HOTTEST CURRY

MADRAS CURRY

SERVES

—— 4 ——

No one, not even Indians, starts life enjoying the heat of chillies. One has to acclimatize to heat, slowly and surely, building up a tolerance, which converts to an enjoyment of heat. And the facts are that spices are addictive – mildly and harmlessly – but addictive none the less. So, once you take your first korma, are you on the road to a phal? It seems that some of us are, some not. But the chances are that your heat tolerance will build up considerably over your curry life-time. The British curry house realized this early on and invented three curries not resembling anything found in India. Hot (Madras), hotter (vindaloo), and hottest (phal). Here, as at the restaurant, I give one method (for Madras) which, with minor adjustments, becomes vindaloo or phal. Two things left to say. Firstly, you can cut back on the chilli to introduce yourself to this curry. Secondly, if you do find food too chillie-hot – try to avoid drinking copious quantities of water. Milk or yoghurt is a better fire extinguisher.

Pre-heat the oven to 190°C/375°F/Gas 5.

Heat the oil in the casserole pot. Stir-fry the garlic for 30 seconds. Add the curry paste, mustard and chilli powder and stir-fry for 30 seconds more. Now add the onion and a few spoonfuls of tomato soup (to keep things mobile). Stir-fry for 5 minutes or so. Stir in the meat and put the lidded casserole into the oven. Stir after 20 minutes, adding the remaining soup, the chillies (if using), and the pepper. After 20 more minutes, add the tomatoes, cream, ground almonds and fresh leaves. After 10 more minutes, taste-test for tenderness. It should be about right, having now had 50 minutes in the oven. Add the garam masala and salt to taste. Allow it to rest for 5–10 minutes then serve.

INGREDIENTS

UTENSILS
lidded casserole pot (see page 12)
PREPARATION TIME
5 minutes
COOKING TIME
55 minutes–1 hour

3 tablespoons vegetable oil
4–6 cloves garlic, finely chopped
2 tablespoons curry paste
1 teaspoon mustard powder
1 teaspoon extra hot chilli powder
225 g (8 oz) onion, as finely chopped as possible
100 ml (3¹/₂ fl oz) tinned cream of tomato soup
750 g (1¹/₂ lb) stewing lamb, in 4 cm (1¹/₂ inch) cubes
1–2 whole fresh green chillies (optional)
2 tablespoons chopped red pepper
3–4 cherry tomatoes, chopped
50 ml (2 fl oz) single cream
2 tablespoons ground almonds
1 tablespoon chopped fresh coriander leaves
1 teaspoon garam masala
Salt to taste

VINDALOO CURRY

SERVES

— 4 —

UTENSILS
lidded casserole pot (see page 12)
PREPARATION TIME
5 minutes
COOKING TIME
55 minutes–1 hour

3 tablespoons vegetable oil
4–6 cloves garlic, finely chopped
2 tablespoons curry paste
1 teaspoon mustard powder
2 teaspoons extra hot chilli powder
225 g (8 oz) onion, as finely chopped as possible
100 ml (3¹/₂ fl oz) tinned cream of tomato soup
550 g (1¹/₄ lb) stewing lamb, in 4 cm (1¹/₂ inch) cubes
1 large baking potato, peeled and cut into large chunks
1–2 whole fresh green chillies (optional)
2 tablespoons chopped red pepper
3–4 cherry tomatoes, chopped
2 tablespoons ground almonds
1 tablespoon chopped fresh coriander leaves
1 teaspoon garam masala
Salt to taste

Pre-heat the oven to 190°C/375°F/Gas 5.

Heat the oil in the casserole pot. Stir-fry the garlic for 30 seconds. Add the curry paste, mustard and chilli powder and stir-fry for 30 seconds more. Now add the onion and a few spoonfuls of tomato soup (to keep things mobile). Stir-fry for 5 minutes or so. Stir in the meat and add the potato. Put the lidded casserole into the oven. Stir after 20 minutes, adding the remaining soup, the chillies (if using), and the pepper. After 20 more minutes, add the tomatoes, ground almonds and fresh leaves. After 10 more minutes, taste-test for tenderness. It should be about right, having now had 50 minutes in the oven. Add the garam masala and salt to taste. Allow it to rest for 5–10 minutes then serve.

PHAL CURRY

SERVES

— 4 —

Pre-heat the oven to 190°C/375°F/Gas 5.

Heat the oil in the casserole pot. Stir-fry the garlic for 30 seconds. Add the curry paste, mustard, chilli powder and the chopped chillies and stir-fry for 30 seconds more. Now add the onion and a few spoonfuls of tomato soup (to keep things mobile). Stir-fry for 5 minutes or so. Stir in the meat and put the lidded casserole into the oven. Stir after 20 minutes, adding the remaining soup, the green chillies (if using), and the pepper. After 20 more minutes, add the tomatoes, ground almonds and fresh leaves. After 10 more minutes, taste-test for tenderness. It should be about right, having now had 50 minutes in the oven. Add the garam masala and salt to taste. Allow it to rest for 5–10 minutes then serve.

INGREDIENTS

UTENSILS
lidded casserole pot (see page 12)
PREPARATION TIME
5 minutes
COOKING TIME
55 minutes–1 hour

3 tablespoons vegetable oil
4–6 cloves garlic, finely chopped
2 tablespoons curry paste
1 teaspoon mustard powder
3 teaspoons extra hot chilli powder (or more!)
3–4 fresh red chillies, chopped
225 g (8 oz) onion, as finely chopped as possible
100 ml (3¹/₂ fl oz) tinned cream of tomato soup
750 g (1¹/₂ lb) stewing lamb, in 4 cm (1¹/₂ inch) cubes
1–2 whole fresh green chillies (optional)
2 tablespoons chopped red pepper
3–4 cherry tomatoes, chopped
2 tablespoons ground almonds
1 tablespoon chopped fresh coriander leaves
1 teaspoon garam masala
Salt to taste

MEAT MOGHLAI

S E R V E S

—— 4 ——

UTENSILS
lidded casserole pot (see page 12), karahi or wok
PREPARATION TIME
5 minutes
COOKING TIME
55 minutes minimum

3 tablespoons butter ghee
1 teaspoon fennel seeds
1 teaspoon coriander seeds
1 teaspoon sesame seeds
$^1/_2$ teaspoon wild onion seeds
$^1/_4$ teaspoon fenugreek seeds
1 tablespoon ground coriander
225 g (8 oz) onion, very
    finely chopped
1 tablespoon curry paste
750 g (1$^1/_2$ lb) lean leg of
    veal, 4 cm (1$^1/_2$ inches)
    cubes
150 g (5 oz) natural yoghurt
1 fennel bulb, finely chopped
10 cm (4 inch) cinnamon
    stick
2–3 bay leaves
35–40 shelled, unsalted
    pistachio nuts
$^1/_2$ red pepper, chopped
1 fresh red chilli
4 tablespoons evaporated milk
1 tablespoon chopped fresh
    mint leaves
100 ml (3$^1/_2$ fl oz) double
    cream
2 teaspoons demerara sugar
1 teaspoon garam masala
Salt to taste

FOR THE TARKA

2 tablespoons butter
1 teaspoon white cumin seeds
1 teaspoon black mustard seeds
20 almonds, chopped

The Moghuls were India's most celebrated emperors. Their heyday was during and after the reign of Queen Elizabeth I. Their most famous legacy was Agra's Taj Mahal, built in 1647. Everything about them was rich, including their food, as the restaurant Moghlai interpretation of this dish shows. One Moghul technique is to enliven the dish towards the end of its cooking with the addition of lightly fried items. It is called the Tarka, and we use it here. The ingredients include butter, yoghurt, cream, evaporated milk and nuts. I've chosen veal here because it suits the recipe and it cooks quite quickly.

Pre-heat the oven to 190°C/375°F/Gas 5.

Heat the ghee in the casserole pot. Fry the seeds for 10 seconds then the ground coriander for 1 minute. Add the onion and the curry paste and stir-fry for 5 minutes. Add the veal and stir-fry for 5 more minutes. Now mix in the yoghurt, the fennel, cinnamon stick, bay leaves and place the lidded pot in the oven.

Grind the pistachios, red pepper, red chilli and evaporated milk with a little water in the food processor to achieve a thick pourable paste. After the pot has been in the oven for 15 minutes, remove it and mix in the paste. Return the pot to the oven for a further 20 minutes. Then remove it again and stir in the leaves, cream, sugar, garam masala and salt to taste. A further 10 minutes in the oven (giving a total oven time of 45 minutes) should be enough time to make the veal really tender (but give it longer if it needs it). During this last oven stage we make the tarka. Heat the butter in a small karahi or wok. Stir-fry the seeds and almonds for about 30 seconds. Add this to the pot just prior to serving. Garnish with snipped chives.

MEAT COOKED WITH FRUIT AND NUTS

S E R V E S

—— 4 ——

UTENSILS
*lidded casserole pot (see
page 12)*
PREPARATION TIME
10 minutes
COOKING TIME
about 1 hour

This is a stunning recipe and does not resemble those dreadful canteen curries swimming with fruit salad! No, this is an authentic Indian recipe called Jardaloo Boti and the fruit (dried apricot in this case) is cooked with the meat and cannot be identified apart from its subtle flavour. This dish originated in Persia, but in medieval Britain we used to cook our meat with fruit. The legacy is pork with apple sauce, turkey with cranberry, etc. Note the surprise ingredient towards the end. Not authentic, to add spirits, but I was taught the trick by an Indian friend – and believe me it's good!

Pre-heat the oven to 190°C/375°F/Gas 5.

Heat the oil in the casserole pot. Stir-fry the seeds, star anise, cloves and cardamoms for 10 seconds. Add the garlic and stir-fry it for about 30 seconds. Then add the spring onion and curry paste and continue to stir-fry for about 8 minutes. Stir in the meat, pineapple juice, the cinnamon, and bay leaves and put the pot into the oven. After 20 minutes stir in the dried apricots, herbs and chilli. After a further 20 minutes, add the nuts, ground almonds, garam masala, cream and the brandy. Stir in well. It should be dryish but a little water is probably needed. Cook for about 10 more minutes. (It has now had 50 minutes in the oven.) Salt to taste, then rest it for 10 minutes before serving.

3 tablespoons sesame oil
2 teaspoons sesame seeds
1 teaspoon coriander seeds
¹/₂ teaspoon black cumin seeds
2 star anise
6–8 cloves
6 green cardamoms
6 cloves garlic, thinly sliced
6–8 spring onions, sliced
2 teaspoons curry paste
*750 g (1¹/₂ lb) stewing steak
  or lamb, cut into 4 cm
  (1¹/₂ inch) cubes*
*50 ml (2 fl oz) pineapple
  juice*
*10 cm (4 inch) cinnamon
  stick*
3–4 bay leaves
7–8 dried apricots, chopped
*10–12 fresh mint leaves,
  chopped*
*2 tablespoons chopped fresh
  coriander leaves*
*1 or more whole fresh red
  chillies*
*20–25 whole almonds,
  shelled*
2 tablespoons ground almonds
2 teaspoons garam masala
50 ml (2 fl oz) single cream
50 ml (2 fl oz) brandy
Salt to taste

THAI PORK GREEN CURRY

SERVES

—— 4 ——

INGREDIENTS

UTENSILS
lidded casserole pot (see page 12)
PREPARATION TIME
10 minutes
COOKING TIME
about 1 hour minimum

3 tablespoons sesame oil
6 cloves garlic, thinly sliced
5 cm (2 inch) piece fresh ginger, cut into thin strips
6–8 spring onions, chopped
1 tablespoon curry paste
2 teaspoons fish paste (optional)
2–3 bay leaves
2 tablespoons finely chopped fresh coriander leaves
1–3 fresh green chillies, finely chopped
750 g (1¹/₂ lb) lean leg of pork, cut into 2.5 cm (1 inch) cubes
1 stalk fresh lemon grass
10–12 fresh basil leaves, chopped
6 tablespoons coconut milk powder
1 teaspoon light soy sauce
1 teaspoon white wine vinegar
1 teaspoon sugar
2 tablespoons whole coriander leaves
Salt to taste

Pork is rarely encountered at the Indian restaurant for religious reasons. Pigs are farmed in several non-Muslim areas in the subcontinent. In Catholic Goa, for example, pork is the most popular meat. It is even more popular in Thailand and this curry is typical in fragrance and aroma as well as taste, enhanced by coriander, basil leaves, and chilli, which give it a greenish appearance. Fresh lemon grass is now readily available. If you can get them use dry lime leaves in place of bay. The optional fish paste (the sandwich spread type out of a jar) substitutes for the smelly authentic shrimp paste (kapi) block which is used in Thai cooking. The final result should be quite runny and is a fair representation of Thai cooking.

Pre-heat the oven to 190°C/375°F/Gas 5.

Heat the oil in the casserole pot. Stir-fry the garlic for 30 seconds. Add the ginger and stir-fry for a further 30 seconds. Add the spring onion and curry paste, and stir-fry for 3 more minutes. Stir in the fish paste, bay leaves and finely chopped coriander and chilli, pork and lemon grass and 150 ml (5 fl oz) water. Put the pot in the oven. Stir after 20 minutes. Stir again after a further 20 minutes, this time adding most of the basil leaves, coconut, soy, vinegar and sugar. Add water if it's too dry. Return to the oven for about 15 more minutes, by which time (55 minutes) it should be tender. Add the coriander leaves and the remaining basil. Salt to taste.

Opposite: MEAT MOGHLAI *(page 64),*
WITH TOMATO CHUTNEY *(page 117)*
Overleaf: BAKED SPICY RED MULLET *(page 87),*
SHREDDED CARROT CHUTNEY *(page 119),* SPICY
COURGETTE AND MANGETOUT JAL-FREZI *(page 94),*
CUCUMBER RAITA *(page 122)*

POULTRY AND EGGS

Our familiar domestic chicken evolved from the wild Jungle Fowl, a native to India a thousand years ago. However, chicken is not as readily available in India as it is here. In the absence of factory farms, and scratching around for its living, the Indian chicken is leaner and pricier than its Western counterpart. There the whole bird is used on the bone but minus the skin (poultry must always be curried without its skin). Being tougher, it takes almost as long to cook as meat. Here we prefer boned white breast or brown leg meat. Cut into bite-size pieces it can be stir-fried to succulent readiness in under 20 minutes. Chicken is so inexpensive over here, that we regard it as a staple, rather than the luxury it once was, and still is, in India. And with pundits extolling the health virtues of 'white' meat over red, it is hardly surprising that, at the Indian restaurant, chicken is the most popular ingredient, with Chicken Tikka Masala everyone's favourite curry. Naturally I have included it here, along with five other chicken curries, each with different attributes. The chapter ends with two traditional curries, one from Rajasthan using duck, the other a fragrant Thai curry ideally suited to turkey. Finally, because I did not know where else to put it, I've also included a tasty egg curry. Nearly all the recipes in this chapter are stir-fried.

Opposite: SPICY SPINACH WITH COTTAGE CHEESE *(page 96),*
WITH PAN-FRIED WHITE PARATHA *(page 107)*

BALTI CHICKEN AND MUSHROOM CURRY

UTENSILS
large karahi or wok
PREPARATION TIME
4 minutes
COOKING TIME
17–20 minutes

650 g (1 lb 6 oz) boned and
  skinned chicken breast
3–4 tablespoons butter ghee
$^1/_2$ teaspoon turmeric
1 teaspoon white cumin seeds
1 teaspoon fennel seeds
$^1/_2$ teaspoon wild onion seeds
2 tablespoons chopped red
  pepper
1 tablespoon yellow pepper
1 fresh red chilli, chopped
1 tablespoon curry paste
2 tablespoons garam masala
4 cloves garlic, thinly sliced
2.5 cm (1 inch) piece fresh
  ginger, cut into matchsticks
225 g (8 oz) spring onions,
  white parts thinly sliced,
  green parts chopped into
  rings
4 tinned plum tomatoes
3–4 fresh spinach leaves
2 tablespoons fresh coriander
  leaves
1 tablespoon fresh mint leaves
1 tablespoon fresh basil leaves
6–8 fresh brown mushrooms
2 tablespoons coconut milk
  powder
$^1/_2$ teaspoon roasted white
  cumin seeds
$^1/_2$ teaspoon roasted coriander
  seeds
100 ml (3$^1/_2$ fl oz) cream of
  mushroom soup

SERVES

—— 4 ——

We met the balti-style of cooking on page 57 in the
previous chapter. And here, of course, it is a stir-fry,
which is quite aromatic and herby and a gorgeous brown
colour. Mushrooms are added to give character and colour
to the dish.

Cut the chicken into pieces about 4 cm (1$^1/_2$ inches) in size.
Heat the ghee in your karahi or wok. Stir-fry the turmeric
and seeds for 10 seconds. Chop the peppers and add with
the chilli, then stir-fry for 2 minutes. Add the curry paste,
garam masala, garlic, ginger and spring onion and continue
stir-frying for 3 minutes. Add the chicken pieces and stir-fry
for 5 minutes. Chop the tomatoes and the fresh leaves and
add to the wok. Add a little water to keep things mobile.
Stir-fry for a further 5 minutes. Slice the mushrooms and
add with the coconut, the roasted seeds and soup and then
continue to stir-fry for up to 5 more minutes. Check that
the chicken is cooked right through by cutting the largest
piece in half and seeing no rawness – just even colour. Salt
to taste and serve with lemon wedges.

HERBAL CHICKEN CURRY

S E R V E S

—— 4 ——

Another name for this recipe is jal-frezi – which means dry-fried. It contains the fresh tastes of ginger, chillies and herbs, and is now almost the most popular dish at the restaurant, where sometimes there are more chillies in this dish than chicken. I have suggested a modest level of chilli here (and please don't omit it) to allow the aromas and flavours to burst through, but if you want more chilli... be my guest!

Cut the chicken into pieces about 4 cm (1¹/₂ inches) in size. Heat the ghee in your karahi or wok. Stir-fry the turmeric and the seeds for 10 seconds. Add the peppers and chilli and stir-fry for about 2 minutes. Add the curry paste, garlic, ginger and spring onion and continue stir-frying for 3 minutes. Add the chicken pieces and stir-fry for 5 minutes. Add the tomatoes and the fresh leaves and a little water to keep things mobile. Stir-fry for a further 5 minutes. Add the garam masala, sugar and Worcestershire sauce and continue to stir-fry for up to 5 more minutes. Check that the chicken is cooked right through by cutting the largest piece in half and seeing no rawness – just even colour. Salt to taste and serve with lemon wedges.

INGREDIENTS

UTENSILS
large karahi or wok
PREPARATION TIME
4 minutes
COOKING TIME
17–20 minutes

750 g (1¹/₂ lb) boned and
  skinned chicken breast
2–3 tablespoons butter ghee
¹/₂ teaspoon turmeric
1 teaspoon white cumin seeds
1 teaspoon fennel seeds
1 tablespoon chopped red
  pepper
1 tablespoon chopped green
  pepper
1 (minimum) fresh green
  chilli, chopped
2 tablespoons curry paste
2 cloves garlic, chopped
5 cm (2 inch) piece fresh
  ginger, chopped
175 g (6 oz) spring onions,
  chopped
6–8 cherry tomatoes, halved
2 tablespoons chopped fresh
  coriander leaves
1 tablespoon chopped fresh
  mint leaves
1 tablespoon garam masala
1 teaspoon brown sugar
¹/₂ teaspoon Worcestershire
  sauce
Salt to taste
Lemon wedges to serve

MALAYAN CHICKEN

S E R V E S

—— 4 ——

UTENSILS
lidded casserole pot (see page 12)
PREPARATION
5 minutes
COOKING TIME
45 minutes

3 tablespoons sesame oil

2 teaspoons sesame seeds

1 teaspoon mustard seeds

¼ teaspoon fenugreek seeds

6 cloves garlic, sliced

5 cm (2 inch) piece fresh ginger, chopped

175 g (6 oz) spring onions, chopped

1½ tablespoons curry paste

400 ml (14 fl oz) tinned coconut milk

200 ml (7 fl oz) water

4 chicken legs, skinned

1 teaspoon dark soy sauce

4–6 baby sweetcorn

6–8 fresh basil leaves, chopped

6 pineapple chunks (optional)

Salt to taste

Snipped chives to garnish

Malaya has a large Indian population, who have developed a curry style unique to the area. It also has many Chinese people, so you'll find a mixture of tastes such as soy sauce and curry paste. This recipe is typical. The whole chicken leg is used this time, including the thigh and the drumstick. Again it is best cooked in the oven in the casserole dish because the end result is quite runny. The use of pineapple is optional, giving a sweetish taste. The tinned coconut milk makes the sauce really easy, and most of the cooking time is waiting anyway. For those with an electric 'slow-cooker' this recipe is just for you. Serve with rice.

Pre-heat the oven to 190°C/375°F/Gas 5.

Heat the oil in the casserole pot and fry the seeds for 10 seconds. Add the garlic and ginger and stir-fry for 30 seconds. Add the spring onion and the curry paste and stir-fry for 3–4 minutes. Add the coconut milk and half fill the can again with the 200 ml (7 fl oz) water. Add to the pot too and, when simmering, put in the chicken pieces, ensuring they are immersed. Put the lidded casserole pot into the oven. After 20 minutes, stir in the soy sauce, baby sweetcorn, fresh leaves and the pineapple pieces. After another 20 minutes (40 minutes total oven time) the chicken should be fully cooked. Test there is no sign of rawness. Salt to taste. Serve garnished with snipped chives.

CHICKEN TIKKA MASALA

S E R V E S
—— 4 ——

Without a shadow of doubt, this is the most popular dish at the curry house. Chicken Tikka already tastes superlative, if not supreme, and adding it to a creamy tangy tandoori sauce was a remarkable master stroke. Of course the best things in life aren't labour-free, and you will need to work a little harder for this recipe than most in the book. Firstly, you have to make the Chicken Tikkas in the recipe on page 52. Before they go under the grill, make the gravy and, since we're doing the job properly, let's use the food processor to obtain a purée texture (omitting this stage if you must, will not affect taste, only texture). You'll adore the results so do have a go please.

———

Cut the chicken into pieces averaging 3–4 cm (1¼ to 1½ inches). Put three-quarters of the double quantity of marinade into a large non-metallic bowl, immerse the chicken in it and, if you have time, marinate it, covered in the fridge, for up to 60 hours (fresh chicken only) and 24 hours (frozen and thawed chicken). Otherwise, proceed by slipping an equal amount of chicken on to each of the 6 skewers and set aside. Pre-heat the grill to medium heat.

Start the stir-fry next. Heat the ghee in the karahi or wok. Stir-fry the seeds for 10 seconds. Add the garlic and stir-fry for 30 seconds. Add the onion and stir-fry for about another 3 minutes. Now add the peppers, chilli, fenugreek, the remaining marinade and stir-fry, sizzling, for 10–12 minutes. Cool and purée in the food processor, if you have time, and bring back to a slow sizzle.

While the karahi ingredients are cooking, put the skewers on to the rack above the foil-lined grill pan and under the grill at the midway position. Grill for 3–4 minutes. Turn and grill for a further 3 minutes or so. Slide the tikkas off their skewers into the simmering karahi ingredients. Stir-fry for about 3 minutes. Add the cream, garam masala, fresh leaves, coconut and mango chutney. Stir-fry for a final 5 minutes or so, checking that the chicken is cooked right through (by cutting a piece in half) before salting to taste.

INGREDIENTS

UTENSILS
large karahi or wok, foil-lined grill pan with rack, 6 skewers, large non-metallic mixing bowl
MARINATION TIME
nil–60 hours
PREPARATION TIME
10 minutes
COOKING TIME
25 minutes minimum

———

750 g (1½ lb) boned and skinned chicken breast

2 × quantity Tandoori Marinade (see page 45)

3 tablespoons butter ghee

1½ teaspoons white cumin seeds

¾ teaspoon fennel seeds

4–6 cloves garlic, chopped

225 g (8 oz) onion, finely chopped

1 tablespoon finely chopped red pepper

1 tablespoon finely chopped green pepper

1–2 fresh green chillies, chopped

1 teaspoon dried fenugreek leaves

50 ml (2 fl oz) single cream

2 teaspoons garam masala

1 tablespoon chopped fresh coriander leaves

1 tablespoon chopped fresh mint leaves

1 tablespoon coconut milk powder

1 tablespoon mango chutney, chopped

Salt to taste

MADRAS CHICKEN

S E R V E S
—— 4 ——

UTENSILS
large karahi or wok
PREPARATION TIME
5 minutes
COOKING TIME
20 minutes

750 g (1½ lb) boned and
  skinned chicken breast
3 tablespoons sunflower oil
4 cloves garlic, chopped
2 tablespoons curry paste
1 teaspoon mustard powder
1 teaspoon extra hot chilli
  powder
225 g (8 oz) onion, finely
  chopped
2 tablespoons chopped green
  pepper
1–2 fresh red chillies, chopped
100 ml (3½ fl oz) tinned
  cream of tomato soup
5–6 cherry tomatoes, halved
50 ml (2 fl oz) single cream
1 tablespoon ground almonds
2 teaspoons garam masala
2 tablespoons chopped fresh
  coriander leaves
Salt to taste

We met the restaurant Madras curry on page 61 in its meat form. As it is so popular, here it is using chicken and the karahi or wok on the stove top. By using this method, but making the adjustments to ingredients according to pages 62 and 63 you can also make the hotter chicken vindaloo and hottest chicken phal.

Cut the chicken breast into pieces averaging 3–4 cm (1¼–1½ inches). Heat the oil and stir-fry the garlic for 30 seconds. Add the curry paste, mustard and chilli powder and stir-fry for 30 seconds more. Now add the onion, peppers and fresh chillies and a few spoonfuls of tomato soup, to keep things mobile. Stir-fry for 4 minutes or so. Add the chicken and stir-fry for a further 5 minutes. Add the remaining soup, tomatoes, cream, ground almonds, garam masala and fresh leaves. Simmer for at least 10 more minutes or until the chicken is cooked right through. Cut a piece to make sure there is no sign of rawness. Salt to taste and serve.

MINCED CHICKEN CURRY

S E R V E S

—— 4 ——

When we think mince, it is usually beef which comes to mind. Actually, any flesh can be minced including any meat or fowl. If you have the time and an electric or hand mincer (see page 14) it is easy and better (for quality) to make your own mince. You can avoid all unwanted matter such as gristle and excess fat, for example.

Chicken flesh minces well (leg or breast) and it cooks quickly. It is available from butchers who will prepare it for you if you ask them. You must obviously use boned chicken and (less obviously) discard the skin.

Heat the ghee and stir-fry the seeds, cardamoms, cassia and cloves for 30 seconds. Add the garlic and curry paste and stir-fry for 30 seconds more. Add the onion, tomato purée, pepper and chilli and stir-fry for about 4 minutes. Add the mince and fenugreek. When it is sizzling, lower the heat to maintain a gentle sizzle while occasionally stirring for about 10 minutes. Add the mushroom soup, the tomatoes, leaves and garam masala. Stir-fry for a further 10 minutes. Salt to taste and serve.

INGREDIENTS

UTENSILS
large karahi or wok
PREPARATION TIME
5 minutes
COOKING TIME
25 minutes

3 tablespoons butter ghee
1 teaspoon white cumin seeds
1 teaspoon black mustard seeds
6 green cardamoms, crushed
5 cm (2 inch) piece cassia bark
4–5 cloves
4–6 cloves garlic, chopped
2 tablespoons curry paste
225 g (8 oz) onion, finely chopped
1 tablespoon tomato purée
2 tablespoons chopped green pepper
1–2 fresh green chillies, chopped
750 g (1¹/₂ lb) minced chicken
2 teaspoons dry fenugreek leaves
100 ml (3¹/₂ fl oz) tinned cream of mushroom soup
4–5 tinned plum tomatoes
2 tablespoons chopped fresh coriander leaves
1 tablespoon garam masala
Salt to taste

THAI RED FRAGRANT TURKEY CURRY

S E R V E S
—— 4 ——

INGREDIENTS

UTENSILS
large karahi or wok
PREPARATION TIME
5 minutes
COOKING TIME
30 minutes

750 g (1½ lb) boned and skinned turkey breast and/or leg meat

3 tablespoons sunflower or soya oil

6 cloves garlic, sliced

5 cm (2 inch) piece fresh ginger, cut into strips

175 g (6 oz) red onion, finely sliced

1 teaspoon Tandoori Paste (see page 44)

1 tablespoon curry paste

1 tablespoon tomato purée

2 teaspoons paprika

½ teaspoon chilli powder

3 tablespoons finely chopped red pepper

3–4 red chillies, chopped

5–6 tinned plum tomatoes, chopped

1 stalk fresh lemon grass

1½ teaspoons light soy sauce

½ teaspoon Worcestershire sauce

400 ml (14 fl oz) tinned coconut milk

10–12 fresh basil leaves, chopped

Salt to taste

Turkey meat is now widely available all year round in the butchery department. As an alternative to chicken, it makes an interesting change. It is much cheaper, but is slightly tougher and takes a little longer to cook. As with chicken it must be cooked thoroughly (there must be no 'rare' centre). As with the Thai curry recipe on page 66 I have modified the ingredients to avoid the hard-to-get items. I should mention that Thais like hot curries, and part of the red colouring comes from red chillies. If you do wish to step down their quantity (but don't omit them altogether), step up the red pepper quantity.

Cut the turkey into bite-size pieces. Heat the oil in the karahi or wok. Stir-fry the garlic and ginger for a minute. Add the onion and stir-fry for a couple more minutes. Add the tandoori paste, curry paste, tomato purée, paprika and chilli powder with just enough water to make things mobile and stir-fry for about 5 minutes more. Add the turkey pieces, the pepper, chillies, tomatoes and lemon grass and stir-fry for another 10 minutes. Add the soy and Worcestershire sauces, the coconut milk, and most of the basil leaves. Simmer for 10–12 minutes. Add the remaining basil leaves. Salt to taste and serve.

RAJASTHANI DUCK CURRY

S E R V E S

—— 4 ——

INGREDIENTS

UTENSILS
lidded casserole pot (see page 12)
PREPARATION TIME
10 minutes
COOKING TIME
1 hour

Rajasthan means the land of the kings. The area is in north-west India. It is home to countless fairy-tale fortresses, perched inaccessibly on mountain tops, or looming alluringly out of deserted deserts. Long since abandoned, their stories and their rajahs are the legends of history. The people remain, and nowhere in India are they more colourful. And nowhere are Indian recipes more exciting than Rajasthan. Wild ducks are still plentiful there. For simplicity I have used duck breast for this recipe. Removing the skin and fat is a chore but the resulting tasty red meat cannot be equalled when curried, especially using the oven and the casserole pot.

———

Pre-heat the oven to 190°C/375°F/Gas 5.

Cut the duck breast into bite-sized pieces. Heat the ghee in the casserole pot. Fry the seeds, cardamoms, cloves, star anise and mace for 30 seconds. Add the garlic and ginger and stir-fry for about a minute. Add the onion and the curry paste and continue stir-frying for about 5 minutes. Add the duck breast and keep turning the pieces until they are seared on all sides (a couple of minutes). Add the cinnamon and bay leaves and a cupful of water and bring to the simmer. Then put the lidded casserole pot into the oven.

After 25 minutes stir in the vichyssoise soup, the fresh leaves, fenugreek and mint. Return to the oven and inspect again after a further 15 minutes. Stir in the cream, saffron and garam masala. It should be quite creamy in texture, but if it does need a little water to achieve this, now is the time. After a further 10 minutes in the oven (total oven time 50 minutes) remove any floating oil (keep it for stock) and stir it well. Salt to taste. Rest it for a few minutes then serve, garnished with chives and almond flakes.

750 g (1½ lb) boned and skinned duck breast
2 tablespoons butter ghee
1 teaspoon white cumin seeds
⅔ teaspoon fennel seeds
⅓ teaspoon fenugreek seeds
6 green cardamoms
2 brown cardamoms
5–6 cloves
2–3 star anise
1 blade mace
4 cloves garlic, sliced
5 cm (2 inch) piece fresh ginger, chopped
225 g (8 oz) onion, finely chopped
2 teaspoons curry paste
10 cm (4 inch) cinnamon stick
4–5 bay leaves
100 ml (3½ fl oz) tinned cream of vichyssoise soup
1 tablespoon chopped fresh coriander leaves
1 teaspoon dried fenugreek leaves
1 teaspoon dried mint leaves
50 ml (2 fl oz) single cream
20–25 strands saffron
1 tablespoon garam masala
Salt to taste
Snipped chives to garnish
Almond flakes to garnish

EGG CURRY WITH SWEETCORN

SERVES

—— 4 ——

INGREDIENTS

UTENSILS
large karahi or wok, medium
saucepan
PREPARATION TIME
4 minutes
COOKING TIME
15–20 minutes

12 quail eggs
3 tablespoons vegetable ghee
2 teaspoons white cumin seeds
4 cloves garlic, finely chopped
2 tablespoons curry paste
175 g (6 oz) spring onions,
    thinly sliced
2 tablespoons finely chopped
    red pepper
1 fresh green chilli, chopped
1 tablespoon tomato purée
2–3 tinned plum tomatoes,
    chopped
1 teaspoon dried fenugreek
    leaves
25–30 fresh coriander leaves
1 large chicken egg
300 g (11 oz) tinned
    sweetcorn and its liquid
Salt to taste
Garam masala to garnish
Snipped chives to garnish

Well it has to be in this chapter, doesn't it? And as to the argument about which came first it is settled! The egg comes last in this chapter… but by no means least. It makes an excellent curry subject. Mind you it doesn't have to be chicken egg. Duck egg works very well too, its extra richness standing up well to curry spicing. But for something rather more dainty (and much quicker too) how about the tiny quail egg? It's a pretty package (and there are few ingredients more cleverly packaged than the egg). And its size makes it tidier to eat than its larger cousins. But note the secondary use of egg in this recipe. Scrambling gives an interesting background texture. The sweetcorn adds an interesting taste. You have to boil the quail eggs first – and there's nothing easier than boiling an egg, so they say! So have a go, please, at this rather special curry. It goes well with rice, of course, but try it with a crunchy French stick.

To boil the quail eggs, bring a medium saucepan half full of water to the boil. The quail eggs should be at room temperature (to prevent cracking). Prick the blunt end of the eggs with a pin (it allows the air to escape and also prevents cracking). Put the eggs into the boiling water. Remove them after exactly 4 minutes. They are now hard-boiled, with no blue ring. Shell them under a running cold tap. Meanwhile, heat the ghee in the karahi or wok. Fry the seeds for 10 seconds. Add the garlic and stir-fry for 30 seconds. Add the curry paste and stir-fry that for about a minute. Add the spring onion, the pepper and chilli, stir-frying for about 8 minutes. Add the tomato purée, tomatoes, the fenugreek and the fresh leaves and stir to the simmer. Add sufficient water to make things mobile then put the hard-boiled eggs in to the karahi or wok along with the raw chicken egg and the sweetcorn with its liquid. Stir gently so that the chicken egg scrambles and everything heats up. Salt to taste. Serve sprinkled with garnishes.

FISH AND SEAFOOD

India's vast coastline and her immense mileage of rivers and lakes add up to an extensive fishing industry, with an enormous wealth of fish and shellfish for which innumerable wonderful recipes have been developed all over the subcontinent. Indians not only relish fish, they enjoy the heads and tail and sucking on the bones and all. We Westerners are rather reticent about such delights. Indeed we appear to dislike fish altogether if it isn't battered and accompanied by chips. It's hardly surprising that our curry houses virtually choose to ignore everything except prawns. But we've never had such good choice at the fish counter and, with fish being so good for us, it is a pleasure to report that nothing makes fish taste better than light spicing. To prove it, I have selected six curry recipes, each using a different popular fish (lemon sole, cod, rainbow trout, John Dory, red mullet and pomfret). Each is cooked in a different way (poaching, stir-frying, grilling, pan-frying, baking and steaming). The remaining three recipes involve prawns and crab, and include a particular favourite of mine – a fragrant Goan recipe. In fact all nine recipes are well worth trying.

LEMON SOLE MOULI

SERVES

—— 4 ——

UTENSILS
large frying-pan
PREPARATION
3 minutes
COOKING TIME
8–11 minutes

2 tablespoons sunflower or
  soya oil
1¹/₂ teaspoons black mustard
  seeds
¹/₂ teaspoon black peppercorns
¹/₂ teaspoon green peppercorns
  in brine
6 cloves garlic, very finely
  chopped
¹/₂ teaspoon turmeric
400 ml (14 fl oz) tinned
  coconut milk
4 lemon sole fillets, each
  about 200 g (7 oz)
6–7 fresh basil leaves,
  chopped
Salt to taste
Snipped chives to garnish
Lime wedges or slices to serve

The mouli method of cooking (also called mollee) comes from South India. Its delicate spicing suits fish particularly well. A short initial fry of mustard seeds and turmeric gives the coconut milk a bright pale yellow colour. Any white flat fish is perfect. Here I've used lemon sole. Served with rice in the traditional way, or with potatoes as a Western alternative.

Heat the oil in the frying-pan. Fry the seeds and peppercorns for 10 seconds. Add the garlic, stir-frying it for 30 seconds. Add the turmeric and stir it into the sizzling oil. Immediately add the coconut milk, stirring it to a gentle simmer.

Add the fish and simmer for 5–8 minutes (depending on the thickness of the sole). Add the leaves and salt to taste. Simmer for just another minute, then garnish with chives and serve with lime wedges or slices.

COD TIKKA MASALA

S E R V E S

—— 4 ——

This is one of my quick curries using frozen cod steaks. You know the ones, they come in regular rectangular packets. Thawed and cut into chunks, there are no bones, and they are really easy to cook, especially if you happen to have some Tandoori Marinade already made up in the fridge. Fish cooks in minutes, and this stir-fry is ready in next to no time.

Heat the oil and stir-fry the seeds for 10 seconds. Add the onion, pepper and chilli and stir-fry for about 3 minutes. Add the marinade and simmer it for about another 3 minutes during which time it will thicken and change colour. Cut the cod into bite-sized cubes and carefully add them to the pan, along with the cream and the tomatoes. Carefully stir-fry for about 8 minutes. Add the leaves, garam masala and salt to taste. Simmer for two more minutes then serve.

INGREDIENTS

UTENSILS
large karahi or wok
PREPARATION TIME
3 minutes
COOKING TIME
10–12 minutes

2 tablespoons vegetable oil
1 teaspoon white cumin seeds
$^1/_2$ teaspoon lovage seeds
175 g (6 oz) onion, very finely chopped
2 tablespoons finely chopped red pepper
1 fresh green chilli, chopped
200 g (7 oz) Tandoori Marinade (see page 45)
750 g (1$^1/_2$ lb) filleted and skinned cod steaks
50 ml (2 fl oz) single cream
2–3 tinned plum tomatoes, chopped
1 tablespoon chopped fresh coriander leaves
2 teaspoons garam masala
Salt to taste

GRILLED SPICY RAINBOW TROUT

SERVES
— 4 —

UTENSILS
foil-lined grill pan and rack, large mixing bowl
PREPARATION TIME
10 minutes
COOKING TIME
11–15 minutes

4 fresh rainbow trout, each about 350 g (12 oz), cleaned and gutted
3–4 tablespoons freshly squeezed lemon juice

FOR THE COATING

SAUCE

2 tablespoons sesame oil
1 teaspoon sesame seeds
4 cloves garlic, very finely chopped
2 tablespoons curry paste
150 g (5 oz) natural Greek yoghurt
50 ml (2 fl oz) double cream
1 teaspoon dried mint
1 teaspoon dried fenugreek leaves
¹/₂ teaspoon salt

FOR DABBING

About 75 g (6 oz) gram flour or cornflour
1 tablespoon garam masala

TO GARNISH

Salt
Chilli powder

Because trout is an oily fish, I find that grilling is one of the best methods of currying it. The result is crispy and dry and very spicily tasty. All that is needed is a couple of minutes to make a coating sauce and a short burst under the grill. Equally good like this are herring, mackerel, pilchard and sardine (small young pilchards). Great with a squeeze of lemon or lime, a salad and crusty fresh bread.

Pre-heat the grill to medium heat.

Wash the fish inside out. It's on the bone with its scales in place, but you can de-head it if you prefer. Massage each fish with lemon juice, then set aside in the fridge. Make the coating sauce by mixing the ingredients with a little water, as needed, in a large mixing bowl. Then immerse the fish in it.

Mix the dabbing ingredients together. Dab the fish on to the flour mixture then place them on to the rack on the foil-lined grill pan, and under the grill at the midway position. Grill for about 6–7 minutes. Turn the fish. Pour on left-over coating sauce and grill for a further 5–8 minutes. Exact timing depends on the fish size. When fully cooked it should look crispy and a little flaky. Sprinkle salt and chilli powder over the fish and serve.

BOMBAY POMFRET

S E R V E S

—— 4 ——

Pomfret is a warm-water exotic fish, available over here all year, fresh and frozen. This is a particularly 'green' recipe both in the health department and in appearance, and it is a traditional Parsee Bombay recipe. It is much easier to make than it sounds and, believe me, is well worth it. Substitute flounder or plaice if you cannot get pomfret. The weight of fish given is after filleting, skinning and de-heading. Serve with bread or rice.

———

Mulch the coating ingredients down in the food processor using water as needed to achieve a thickish mouldable purée. Using all the purée, cover each piece of fish on both sides with it, then wrap each one loosely in cooking foil. Bring water in the double boiler or steamer to the boil. You can improvise using a large saucepan with a close-fitting metal sieve (which must not touch the water) with a lid on top. Put the foil-covered fish into the sieve or steamer basket and cover and steam for 10 minutes. Remove the steamer and rest the fish for 5–10 minutes (this finishes off the process). Carefully unwrap the foil. The coating should have penetrated the fish, adhering in places to its surface. Transfer each fish to a serving plate, pouring any juices over it and scraping on any loose cooked coating. Garnish with the coconut and lime wedges and serve.

INGREDIENTS

UTENSILS
food processor, double boiler, steamer or sieve over a saucepan
PREPARATION TIME
10 minutes
COOKING TIME
15 minutes and 5–10 minutes resting

FOR THE COATING
10 tablespoons chopped fresh coriander leaves and tender stalks
4 tablespoons chopped fresh mint leaves
4–6 fresh spinach leaves, coarsely chopped
1 tablespoon chopped green pepper
1–3 fresh green chillies, chopped
4 cloves garlic, quartered
4–6 spring onions, chopped
¹/₂ teaspoon salt
2 tablespoons vinegar (any type)
4 tablespoons natural Greek yoghurt

4 pieces of prepared pomfret, each weighing about 225 g (8 oz)
Dessicated coconut to garnish
Lime wedges to garnish

PAN-FRIED CURRIED FISH

S E R V E S
—— 4 ——

UTENSILS
large flat frying-pan
PREPARATION TIME
3 minutes
COOKING TIME
8–11 minutes

2 tablespoons sesame oil

2 teaspoons black mustard
  seeds

$^1/_4$ teaspoon lovage seeds

$^1/_4$ teaspoon wild onion seeds

1 teaspoon ground coriander

1 teaspoon paprika

$^1/_2$ teaspoon turmeric

$^1/_4$ teaspoon mango powder

4 teaspoons chilli powder

4 cloves garlic, sliced

1 tablespoon chopped red
  pepper

1 fresh whole green chilli,
  chopped

1 tablespoon tomato purée

6 cherry tomatoes, chopped

1 tablespoon chopped fresh
  coriander leaves

2 tablespoons butter

750 g (1$^1/_2$ lb) John Dory
  fillets

50 g (2 oz) creamed coconut
  block

120 ml (4 fl oz) boiling
  water

About 20 shelled, unsalted
  pistachio nuts, chopped

Snipped chives to garnish

I've chosen John Dory for this recipe because it is easily available and works well in this recipe. Although it is a round fish it is available in filleted slices, suitable for pan-frying. Alternatively you can use any filleted flat fish. Serve with bread or rice.

Heat the oil in the large frying-pan. Stir-fry the seeds for 10 seconds. Add the ground spices and stir-fry them for 20 seconds. Add a spoonful or two of water then the garlic and stir-fry the mixture for 30 seconds more. Add the pepper, chilli, tomato purée, tomatoes, leaves and butter and bring to the sizzle. Now place the fish fillets into the pan and work them around so that the mixture integrates with them. Fry for 3–5 minutes. During this time put the coconut into a small mixing bowl or jug, add about 120 ml (4 fl oz) of boiling water from the kettle to the coconut. Stir to melt it. Turn the fish over, pour the coconut into the pan. Fry for a further 4–5 minutes. Garnish with the chopped nuts and chives and serve.

BAKED SPICY RED MULLET

SERVES
—— 4 ——

Mediterranean red mullet is an ugly brute. It always seems to me that it is wearing a stocking mask! That aside, it tastes good, it is readily available, and you can request that the fishmonger de-heads it while gutting it for you. Its colour and flavour suit this tandoori-influenced recipe. Serve with lemon wedges, salad, chutneys and crusty bread.

Pre-heat the oven to 190°C/375°F/Gas 5.

Foil-line an oven tray. Wash the fish inside and out. Massage with the lime juice and set aside. Mix the coating sauce ingredients in a mixing bowl with enough water to make a thick but just pourable paste. Arrange the fish, on their sides on the tray, so that they are touching intimately and coat with half the sauce. Put them into the oven and bake for 10 minutes. Turn them and coat with the remaining sauce and bake for a further 5 minutes. The fish should now be cooked, but as ovens vary enormously you must decide for yourself. The coating should be crispy but not about to burn. Nor should it still be wettish and pale-coloured. The flesh should come easily off the bone. Chances are it needs a few minutes longer – possibly with the oven turned off.

INGREDIENTS

UTENSILS
foil-lined oven tray
PREPARATION TIME
5 minutes
COOKING TIME
15–20 minutes

4 red mullet, each weighing about 450–500 g (1 lb–1 lb 2 oz) before de-heading and gutting
Juice of 2–3 fresh limes

FOR THE COATING

SAUCE

6 cloves garlic, finely chopped
100 g (4 oz) onion, very finely chopped
1–2 fresh green chillies, finely chopped
1 tablespoon tomato purée
400 g (14 oz) Tandoori Marinade (see page 45)
2 tablespoons curry paste
1 teaspoon tamarind powder (optional)
$^1/_2$ teaspoon salt

CRAB AND SHRIMP CURRY

SERVES

—— 4 ——

UTENSILS
large karahi or wok
PREPARATION TIME
3 minutes
COOKING TIME
10 minutes

2 tablespoons sesame oil
1 teaspoon sesame seeds
1 teaspoon mustard seeds
1 teaspoon fennel seeds
$^1/_2$ teaspoon black cumin seeds
175 g (6 oz) spring onions,
   sliced
1$^1/_2$ tablespoons curry paste
1 tablespoon tomato purée
200 g (7 oz) frozen white
   crabmeat, thawed
100 g (4 oz) frozen brown
   crabmeat, thawed
350 g (12 oz) standard
   cooked, peeled prawns,
   thawed if frozen
75 g (3 oz) cooked frozen
   peas
50 ml (2 fl oz) single cream
1 tablespoon chopped fresh
   coriander leaves
1 tablespoon garam masala
Salt to taste

There are some very tempting ingredients at the fish-monger's counter these days. Fresh crab and prawns always look wonderful to me. It's something to do with the pink colour, I think. My wife Dominique doesn't agree; her adoration of the colour pink borders on the fanatical, but any kind of shell-fish she really doesn't enjoy – pink colour notwithstanding. It's nothing to do with allergy either – she simply does not like the look of them. They are ugly – all those tentacles (she says!). I mention all this because you need to be sure that you have a consensus amongst your diners before featuring this dish. If you have, it's a winner and, using frozen crabmeat and prawns, their colour enhanced with the green of the peas, it's one of the quickest and easiest hot dishes in this book. Serve with nothing more than plain rice and a fresh mint chutney.

Although it is better to thaw the crabmeat and the prawns in advance (in the fridge in covered bowls for 24 hours), if you don't do this the recipe will still work. Simply take more time on a lower heat stir-frying until the crab and prawns have thawed.

———

Heat the oil in your karahi or wok and stir-fry the seeds for 10 seconds. Add the spring onion and stir-fry for about 3 minutes. Add the curry paste and tomato purée, and continue the stir-fry for another 3 minutes. Now add the crabmeat, prawns, and the peas, and stir-fry for a further 3 minutes. Add the cream, leaves, and garam masala. Simmer for a minute. Salt to taste and serve.

GOAN FRAGRANT RED PRAWN CURRY

SERVES

—— 4 ——

India's most popular seaside destination is Goa. Formerly a Portuguese colony, and never British, its people are Catholic in religion, Hispanic in background, gregarious in outlook and, though totally Indian in appearance, they are Mediterranean in temperament. And this is never better displayed than in Goan cuisine. This fiery, red, spectacular dish is a typical example – here, for fun, using 2 sizes of prawn (you could make do with one or the other of course). The smooth texture is best achieved by making a purée with the food processor. (Alternatively very finely chop the purée ingredients.) Serve this curry with rice or bread.

———

Put all the purée ingredients into the food processor and pulse it, using just enough water to achieve a porridge consistency.

Heat the oil in the karahi or wok. Stir-fry the seeds and turmeric for 30 seconds, add the purée and stir-fry for around 5 minutes. During this time it will reduce and change colour and will need a little water added as you go, so that it remains at the same consistency right through to the end of cooking. Add the prawns and the tomatoes and stir-fry for 3 more minutes. Add the coconut and leaves and stir-fry for a final 2 minutes. Salt to taste. Garnish with the roasted seeds and lime wedges.

INGREDIENTS

UTENSILS
large karahi or wok
PREPARATION TIME
4 minutes
COOKING TIME
10 minutes

FOR THE PURÉE
50 g (2 oz) fresh red cayenne chillies
1/2 teaspoon (minimum) extra hot chilli powder
1 teaspoon paprika
1 tablespoon tomato purée
75 g (3 oz) raw cashew nuts
1/2 teaspoon tamarind powder or mango powder
1 tablespoon vinegar (any type)
3–4 cloves garlic, halved

4 tablespoons sunflower oil
1 teaspoon white cumin seeds
1 teaspoon mustard seeds
1/2 teaspoon turmeric
450 g (1 lb) standard cooked, peeled prawns
225 g (8 oz) peeled king prawns
2–3 tomatoes, chopped
2 tablespoons coconut milk powder
About 30 fresh coriander leaves
Salt to taste

TO GARNISH
Roasted white cumin seeds
Roasted coriander seeds
Lime wedges

KING PRAWN CHILLI MASALA

SERVES

—— 4 ——

UTENSILS
large karahi or wok
PREPARATION TIME
3 minutes
COOKING TIME
12 minutes

2–3 tablespoons butter ghee

$^1/_2$ teaspoon turmeric

1 teaspoon white cumin seeds

$^1/_2$ teaspoon fennel seeds

$^1/_2$ teaspoon mustard seeds

$^1/_4$ teaspoon lovage seeds

2 teaspoons green peppercorns
in brine

1 tablespoon chopped red
pepper

1 tablespoon chopped green
pepper

1 (minimum) fresh green
chilli, chopped

2 tablespoons curry paste

2 cloves garlic, chopped

5 cm (2 inch) piece fresh
ginger, chopped

175 g (6 oz) spring onions,
chopped

750 g (1$^1/_2$ lb) king prawns,
cooked and peeled

6–8 cherry tomatoes, halved

2 tablespoons chopped fresh
coriander leaves

1 tablespoon chopped fresh
mint leaves

1 tablespoon garam masala

1 teaspoon brown sugar

$^1/_2$ teaspoon Worcestershire
sauce

Salt to taste

Lemon wedges to serve

The previous Goan recipe was a hot one. So is this one but its heat is as different as its appearance. Instead of a hot red purée gravy, here we have a bright yellow one, punctuated by the red and green of the leaves and peppers and chilli. The minimum chilli requirement is one – hot heads will no doubt want more! Note the use of green peppercorns, which also contributes to the heat stakes!

Heat the ghee in the karahi or wok and stir-fry the turmeric and the seeds for 10 seconds. Add the peppercorns, peppers and chilli and stir-fry for about 2 minutes. Add the curry paste, garlic, ginger and spring onion and continue stir-frying for 3 minutes. Add the king prawns and stir-fry for 2 minutes. Add the tomatoes and the fresh leaves and a little water to keep things mobile. Stir-fry for a further 3 minutes and then add the garam masala, sugar and Worcestershire sauce, and continue to stir-fry for 2 more minutes. Salt to taste and serve with lemon wedges.

VEGETABLES AND LENTILS

Contrary to popular belief, only in a few regions, Gujarat in the North-west and Kerala in the South, for example, is the majority of Indians vegetarian by choice. In Muslim areas over 90 per cent are meat eaters. Given the choice most Indians eat meat, poultry or fish curry accompanied by one or more vegetable dishes, plus rice and/or Indian bread. Of course, if you are a vegetarian there is no better way of making your food tasty than by spicing it. As a non-vegetarian, you have greater variety of choice. You can use this chapter to make those all-important vegetable side dishes. Or you can ring the changes from time to time, and have one or more of those dishes as your main meal. These eleven recipes contain many restaurant favourites, and they are quick and easy to make. All of them use vegetables which are readily available. These days supermarkets even do all the preparation for you, and offer interesting ready-to-cook vegetable combinations in glossy packages (albeit at a price). Feel free to use these or substitute any vegetables of your choice in my recipes.

CAULIFLOWER BHAJEE

SERVES

—— 4 as an accompaniment ——

Cauliflower suits the currying process well. Being relatively robust, in texture and flavour, it needs a bold approach. This bhajee (bhajee simply means cooked vegetables) has the tanginess of tamarind with the crunch of roasted seeds, and is very satisfying. Broccoli can be substituted, or you can use half and half cauliflower and broccoli. Either way use only the florets, discarding leaves and most of the pithy stems.

———

Steam, boil or microwave the cauliflower, fennel and Chinese leaves until they are as tender as you like them. Meanwhile heat the oil in the karahi or wok and fry the seeds for 10 seconds. Add the garlic and ground spices and stir-fry for about a minute. Add the curry paste and spring onions and continue to stir-fry for 3–4 more minutes. Add the tomatoes and the cauliflower, fennel and Chinese leaves, mixing in well with a little water. Stir-fry for 2–3 minutes. Salt to taste. Garnish with coriander and roasted seeds and serve.

INGREDIENTS

UTENSILS
large karahi or wok
PREPARATION TIME
5 minutes
COOKING TIME
10 minutes

450 g (1 lb) cauliflower
  florets
225 g (8 oz) fennel bulb,
  chopped
3–4 Chinese leaves, shredded
3 tablespoons sunflower oil
$^1/_2$ teaspoon white cumin
  seeds
$^1/_2$ teaspoon black cumin seeds
$^1/_2$ teaspoon black mustard
  seeds
4 cloves garlic, chopped
1 teaspoon turmeric
1 teaspoon ground coriander
1 teaspoon paprika
$^1/_2$ teaspoon tamarind powder
  or mango powder
1 tablespoon curry paste
4–6 spring onions, shredded
3–4 tinned plum tomatoes
Salt to taste

TO GARNISH
1 tablespoon fresh coriander
  leaves
$^1/_2$ teaspoon roasted coriander
  seeds
$^1/_2$ teaspoon roasted white
  cumin seeds

PAN-FRIED OKRA WITH MANGETOUT

SERVES

—— 4 as an accompaniment ——

The problem with okra (ladies fingers or bindi) is that, after a certain amount of cooking, it produces a sticky sap which they like in India, but which we rather dislike here. The answer is dramatically simple. Just stir-fry them for a short burst, exactly as one does for mangetout. In fact, here I've combined mangetout with okra to give an original but rapid result.

———

Wash the okra and mangetout. Snip the tops and tails off the mangetout. Heat the ghee and butter in the large karahi or wok or flat frying-pan. Stir-fry the seeds for 20 seconds, add the garlic and continue stir-frying for 30 seconds. Then add the onion, red pepper and chilli and give them about 4 more minutes. While the onions are sizzling, cut off and discard the okra stalks and caps, then cut them into 2.5 cm (1 inch) pieces. Put them straight into the karahi with the sugar and briskly stir-fry them to coat them with the oily mixture (and seal them). Add the mangetout and stir-fry until they are as tender as you wish. For me, who likes them very crisp, this takes no more than 4 minutes. Add salt and garam masala to taste. Garnish with the leaves and serve at once.

INGREDIENTS

UTENSILS
large karahi, wok or flat frying-pan
PREPARATION TIME
5 minutes
COOKING TIME
9–10 minutes

16–20 small tender okra
16–20 mangetout
2 tablespoons vegetable ghee
2 tablespoons butter
$^1/_2$ teaspoon black cumin seeds
$^1/_2$ teaspoon fennel seeds
$^1/_2$ teaspoon black mustard seeds
$^1/_2$ teaspoon fenugreek seeds
$^1/_2$ teaspoon wild onion seeds
$^1/_2$ teaspoon sesame seeds
4 cloves garlic, thinly sliced
175 g (6 oz) spring onions, shredded
1 tablespoon finely chopped red pepper
1 or more red chilli, shredded
1 teaspoon white sugar
Salt to taste
Garam masala to taste
1 tablespoon whole coriander leaves to garnish

SPICY COURGETTE AND MANGETOUT JAL-FREZI

SERVES

—— 4 as an accompaniment ——

Courgette (zucchini) and mangetout are not in the traditional Indian vegetable repertoire. I like them because they are quick to cook, staying crispy and fresh, in this simple jal-frezi (stir-fry). I also add tomato, tamarind and coconut here and serve it with Plain Rice (see page 111) and Tarka Dhal (see page 101).

Wash, then snip the tips and tails of the mangetout and the courgettes. Cut the courgettes diagonally and thinly so that they are about the same shape as the mangetout. Heat the oil in the karahi or wok. Stir-fry the seeds, tamarind or mango powder, turmeric and curry paste for about a minute. Add the spring onion, chilli, tomatoes and stir-fry for a couple more minutes. Add the mangetout, courgettes, sugar, coconut, fresh leaves and salt to taste and stir-fry until as tender as you wish – minimum time for maximum crispness is 4 minutes. Add tiny amounts of water, as required, to keep things mobile. Garnish with roasted seeds and serve at once.

INGREDIENTS

UTENSILS
large karahi or wok
PREPARATION TIME
4 minutes
COOKING TIME
8 minutes

16–20 mangetout
5–6 × 10 cm (4 inch)
  courgettes
4 tablespoons sunflower oil
1 teaspoon sesame seeds
1 teaspoon black mustard
  seeds
1/2 teaspoon tamarind powder
  or mango powder
1/2 teaspoon turmeric
1 tablespoon curry paste
4–5 spring onions, shredded
1 fresh red chilli, thinly sliced
4 cherry tomatoes, halved
1 teaspoon white sugar
1 tablespoon coconut milk
  powder
1 tablespoon chopped fresh
  coriander leaves
Salt to taste
Roasted white cumin seeds to
  garnish

SPICY MASHED AUBERGINE

S E R V E S

—— 4 as an accompaniment ——

One package I always admire at the greengrocer's is the aubergine (egg plant or brinjal). Its gleaming blacky-purple boot-shape case looks as though it has been given a 'spit-and-polish', and is ready to go on parade. It's almost a shame to cook it! But I did say 'almost'. In fact Indians enjoy cooked aubergine so much that I'd be remiss if I missed out a suitable recipe.

This is one of my favourite recipes. Traditionally, the aubergine is slowly cooked over coals then its flesh is scooped out and mashed before being curried. Just in case your eyes have glazed over because you've forgotten to light your coals, here's a quick and easy method of achieving more-or-less the same results in quick-march time. This dish will also freeze well.

————

Wash and de-stalk the aubergine. Halve it and immerse it in a large saucepan of boiling water and simmer for 10 minutes (or microwave it on HIGH for 3 minutes). Meanwhile heat the oil in the large karahi or wok and stir-fry the marinade, garam masala and curry paste for 3 minutes. At the same time, in the small karahi heat the ghee and stir-fry the garlic for 30 seconds and the onion, pepper, chilli and leaves for 3–4 minutes.

Scoop out the aubergine flesh, discarding any pithy centre or seeds. Mash the flesh with the potato masher and add it to the large karahi. Stir-fry to the sizzle. Add the contents of the small karahi and the cream, garam masala, and salt to taste. Garnish with seeds and chives and serve.

INGREDIENTS

UTENSILS
large saucepan, large and small karahi or wok, potato masher
PREPARATION TIME
2 minutes
COOKING TIME
10 minutes

450 g (1 lb) aubergine
2 tablespoons vegetable oil
4 teaspoons Tandoori Marinade (see page 45)
2 tablespoons garam masala
2 teaspoons curry paste
2 tablespoons ghee
4 cloves garlic, chopped
100 g (4 oz) onion, finely chopped
2 tablespoons red pepper, finely chopped
1 fresh green chilli, sliced
2 tablespoons chopped fresh basil leaves
1 tablespoon chopped fresh mint leaves
50 ml (2 fl oz) single cream
2 teaspoons garam masala
Salt to taste
Roasted cumin seeds to garnish
Snipped chives to garnish

SPICY SPINACH WITH COTTAGE CHEESE

SERVES

—— 4 as an accompaniment ——

This recipe is a quick version of sag paneer. Paneer is Indian cheese which is not actually difficult to make, but is somewhat messy, and time-consuming, so I have substituted a close relative – cottage cheese. As it comes ready-made in tubs, its slight differences are well out-weighed by its readiness. One of the great combinations is spinach and paneer but although I've 'compromised' the paneer, let's stick to fresh baby spinach leaves for a delightful curry accompaniment.

Wash and coarsely chop the spinach. Microwave or steam it (in a metal sieve over a pan of boiling water) to soften it. A couple of minutes is ample.

Meanwhile heat the ghee in the karahi or wok. Stir-fry the seeds for 10 seconds. Add the garlic and the onion and stir-fry these for a further 2 minutes. Add the curry paste and garam masala and when sizzling add the spinach and mint. Stir-fry for a couple of minutes, to ensure the panful is hot. Then carefully mix in the cottage cheese. Salt to taste. Give it a further minute in the pan then garnish with almonds and serve.

INGREDIENTS

UTENSILS
large saucepan, metal sieve, large karahi or wok
PREPARATION TIME
5 minutes
COOKING TIME
6 minutes

500 g (1 lb 2 oz) fresh baby spinach leaves
4 tablespoons butter ghee
1 teaspoon white cumin seeds
¹/₃ teaspoon fenugreek seeds
2 cloves garlic, chopped
100 g (4 oz) onion, sliced
1 tablespoon curry paste
1 tablespoon garam masala
2 tablespoons chopped fresh mint leaves
75 g (3 oz) cottage cheese
Salt to taste
2 tablespoons chopped flaked almond to garnish

BALTI SWEETCORN, CELERY AND PEAS

SERVES

—— 4 as a main course ——

Balti, as I've mentioned elsewhere in this book, is a quick stir-fry method from North Pakistan. After centuries of nonentity over there, and a decade and a bit of incubation in Birmingham, it swept to fame all over Britain within a year. As I've already said, balti dishes are the 'use-it-up' brigade's perfect recipes. Using a basic aromatic, spicy, herby sauce, you can put almost any ingredient (or combination) you have to hand in the fridge or freezer, left-over or fresh, cooked or raw. I've suggested sweetcorn and celery and peas here – they are quick to cook and attractive in colour – but feel free to substitute any vegetable or pulse of your own choice. The recipe can hold its own as a main dish with just naan bread or chapati and chutneys and dips (notably the Fresh Onion Chutney on page 116 and the Balti Raita on page 121).

———

Heat the ghee in the large karahi or wok. Stir-fry the seeds, cardamoms and cassia bark for 10 seconds. Add the garlic and stir-fry it for 30 seconds, then the ginger for 30 seconds and next the spring onions for 2 minutes. Next, in goes the curry paste, garam masala and yoghurt. Stir-fry these for 2 more minutes. Now add the peppers, chilli, leaves and the celery and stir-fry these for 2 minutes. Add the sweetcorn and liquid, the tomatoes and 2–3 spoons of their liquid, the Worcestershire sauce, mango chutney, coconut powder and the peas. Stir this until it is sizzling (for about a couple of minutes). Salt to taste and serve.

INGREDIENTS

UTENSILS
large karahi or wok
PREPARATION TIME
5 minutes
COOKING TIME
10 minutes

3 tablespoons ghee
1 teaspoon fennel seeds
$^1/_2$ teaspoon black cumin seeds
3–4 cardamoms, crushed
5 cm (2 inch) piece cassia bark
4 cloves garlic, chopped
5 cm (2 inch) cube fresh ginger, chopped
4–5 spring onions, chopped
1 tablespoon curry paste
2 tablespoons garam masala
4 tablespoons natural Greek yoghurt
$^1/_2$ red pepper, chopped
$^1/_2$ yellow pepper, chopped
1 or more green chilli, chopped
2 tablespoons chopped fresh coriander leaves
2 tablespoons finely chopped celery
300 g (11 oz) tinned sweetcorn and liquid
2–3 tinned plum tomatoes and liquid
1 teaspoon Worcestershire sauce
1 tablespoon mango chutney, chopped
2 tablespoons coconut powder
4 tablespoons peas, thawed if frozen
Salt to taste

97

UTENSILS
large karahi or wok
PREPARATION TIME
2 minutes
COOKING TIME
5–6 minutes

200 g (7 oz) tinned red
*   kidney beans*
2 tablespoons sunflower oil
4 cloves garlic, chopped
2 tablespoons curry paste
150 g (5 oz) frozen green
*   beans, thawed*
4 tablespoons houmous
400 g (14 oz) tinned chick
*   peas and their liquid*
2 tablespoons chopped fresh
*   coriander leaves*
Salt to taste
Sesame seeds to garnish

BEAN AND CHILLI MASALA

S E R V E S

—— 4 as a main course ——

Resorting to tinned beans and the freezer, this recipe is what I call a winter warmer. Beans are so full of protein and this dish is filling and tasty enough to suffice as a main course when served with Pullao Rice (see page 112) and chutneys (see page 115). Note the use of houmous which is made with ground chick peas, is readily available at the deli counter and makes a tasty way of thickening the curry.

Discard the kidney bean liquid and rinse the beans. Heat the oil, stir-fry the garlic for 30 seconds. Add the curry paste and stir-fry for a further 30 seconds. Add the kidney beans, green beans, houmous, chick peas and their liquid, and the fresh leaves and simmer for 3–4 minutes. Salt to taste, garnish with seeds and serve.

SOUTH INDIAN VEGETABLE CURRY

S E R V E S

—— 4 as a main course ——

If you haven't tasted South Indian curries, you haven't lived! And you will not get them in the average UK curry house. The runny sauce is a delicious combination of sour (yoghurt), savoury (spices), creamy (coconut milk) and heat (chillies). In the sauce are simmered mixed vegetables. Typically these would be white radish (mooli), broad beans, carrots and two real exotics – drumsticks and karela (long pithy marrow and bitter gourd respectively). These are available but too specialized for quick and easy cooking so I have substituted asparagus tips for drumsticks and courgettes for the gourds. Served with rice and chutneys it is ample and self-sufficient as a main course dish.

———

Heat the oil in the karahi or wok. Fry the seeds for 10 seconds. Stir-fry the turmeric, curry leaves (if using) and dried chilli for 30 seconds. Add the garlic and after a further 30 seconds, add the coconut milk, creamed coconut and yoghurt. Add the remaining ingredients (except the salt and nuts) and simmer for 7–8 minutes. Salt to taste and garnish with the cashews before serving.

INGREDIENTS

UTENSILS
large karahi or wok
PREPARATION TIME
5 minutes
COOKING TIME
9–10 minutes

4 tablespoons sesame oil
1 teaspoon sesame seeds
1 teaspoon black mustard seeds
$^1/_2$ teaspoon turmeric
6–8 curry leaves (if available)
1 teaspoon chopped dried red chillies
6 cloves garlic, sliced
150 ml (5 fl oz) tinned coconut milk
25 g (1 oz) creamed coconut block
100 g (4 oz) natural Greek yoghurt
150 g (5 oz) white radish (mooli), chopped into small cubes
150 g (5 oz) frozen broad beans, thawed
150 g (5 oz) carrot, shredded or thinly chopped
8 fresh asparagus tips
4 × 10 cm (4 inch) courgettes, tips removed and chopped
1 fresh red chilli, chopped
1 fresh green chilli, sliced lengthwise
Salt to taste
10–12 chopped unsalted cashew nuts to garnish

BOMBAY POTATO

S E R V E S

—— 4 as an accompaniment ——

UTENSILS
large karahi or wok
PREPARATION TIME
2 minutes
COOKING TIME
4–5 minutes

3 tablespoons butter ghee
¼ teaspoon lovage seeds
Pinch of wild onion seeds
2–3 cloves garlic, finely
  chopped
75 g (3 oz) onion, very
  finely chopped
1½ tablespoons curry paste
3 tablespoons natural Greek
  yoghurt
2 teaspoons sugar
20–24 baby new potatoes
  (weighing about 500 g/
  1 lb 2 oz), cooked
2–3 plum tomatoes, chopped
1 tablespoon chopped fresh
  coriander leaves
2 teaspoons garam masala
Salt to taste

I visit Bombay once, maybe twice, a year. I meet chefs there and go to many a good restaurant. But try as I may, I have never found a recipe for Bombay Potato. Yet over here all 8000 Indian restaurants in the land serve Bombay Potato with such consistency of standard, that you would think it was a traditional recipe a thousand years old. Of course, it's as much an invention as Madras curry and Bangalore phal. As with all things brilliant, it's simple, effective and a first-class transformation of that son of the soil – the potato. If time is really short, you can use tinned potatoes, but I'd prefer that you use fresh baby new potatoes (now always available). No need to peel – just scrub and boil.

———

Heat the ghee. Fry the seeds for 10 seconds. Stir-fry the garlic for 30 seconds. Add the onion and stir-fry for a further minute. Add the paste, yoghurt and sugar and simmer for a minute. Add the potatoes, tomatoes, leaves and garam masala. Stir-fry for a couple more minutes. Salt to taste and serve.

TARKA DHAL

SERVES

—— 4 ——

Sadly, no one makes tinned unspiced red lentils, so we have to make our own. It's effort-free really. Portion size as an accompaniment is 30 g (just over an ounce) of dry red lentils per person. When cooked it swells by a factor of about 3. The reason for this is that lentils absorb water at the ratio of 2:1. So that's what we need to cook it: twice as much water as lentils (in volume terms), plus a bit more to allow for evaporation. I find half a coffee mug of lentils (around 125 g/4¹/₂ oz) and a full coffee mug of water (around 250 ml/8 fl oz) works perfectly for 4 portions. You may prefer to cook a larger amount and freeze any surplus in small yoghurt pots.

———

Spread out the lentils on a work surface and pick out suspect matter – little particles of grit. Rinse the lentils under the running cold tap for 1 minute, then soak them while you bring the measured water to the boil in a large saucepan. Add the lentils. Stir a few times for the first minute (to prevent the lentils sticking to the bottom of the pan). Leave the lentils to simmer for 20 minutes. Don't put the lid on as this will cause the water to foam over. Depending on the lentils, you may need to spoon off the scum. As lentils also vary in absorption qualities, you may also need to add a little water as you go (boiled water from the kettle) but only do so if it really looks like it is drying up too much.

During this long simmering stage, heat the ghee in the karahi or wok. Fry the seeds for 10 seconds. Add the garlic and onion and, on a low heat, stir-fry for around 10 minutes. Add the curry paste and garam masala and continue slow cooking for a few more minutes. Add the karahi mixture to the lentils with the coconut milk powder, fresh leaves, fenugreek leaves, tomato ketchup and salt to taste. Stir-fry for another 5 minutes minimum. Times are very flexible – you can't overcook this dish – but you can dry it out too much, causing it to stick. So watch that water content. The dish retains heat for ages. It can be cooled or frozen and re-heated (more water is needed then).

INGREDIENTS

UTENSILS
large saucepan and karahi or wok
PREPARATION TIME
3 minutes
COOKING TIME
25 minutes minimum

125 g (4½ oz) red lentils
250 ml (8 fl oz) water
3 tablespoons vegetable ghee
1 teaspoon white cumin seeds
1 teaspoon black mustard seeds
6 cloves garlic, chopped
100 g (4 oz) onion, finely sliced
1 tablespoon curry paste
1 teaspoon garam masala
1 tablespoon coconut milk powder
1 tablespoon chopped fresh coriander leaves
1 teaspoon dry fenugreek leaves
1 tablespoon tomato ketchup
Salt to taste

ALOO GOBI CURRY

SERVES

—— 4 as an accompaniment ——

Gobi is cauliflower and aloo, potato. And the 'hard' cabbage and the root go very well indeed together. Here I've used frozen broccoli in place of cauliflower but you can use both or either. And to tie things together I've used strings of shredded carrot which add taste and colour. As with the previous recipe, I have used tinned potatoes to save time. Again you are welcome to use fresh.

———

Heat the ghee. Fry the seeds for 10 seconds. Stir-fry the garlic for 30 seconds. Add the onion and stir-fry for a couple more minutes. Add the paste, yoghurt and sugar and simmer for a minute. Add the potatoes, broccoli, carrot, leaves and garam masala. Stir-fry for a couple more minutes. Salt to taste and serve.

INGREDIENTS

UTENSILS
large karahi or wok
PREPARATION TIME
2 minutes
COOKING TIME
5–6 minutes

3 tablespoons butter ghee
1 teaspoon white cumin seeds
¼ teaspoon fennel seeds
2–3 cloves garlic, finely chopped
75 g (3 oz) onion, very finely chopped
1½ tablespoons curry paste
3 tablespoons natural Greek yoghurt
2 teaspoons sugar
10–12 baby new potatoes (weighing about 250 g/ 9 oz), cooked
200 g (7 oz) frozen broccoli, thawed and cooked
100 g (4 oz) carrot, shredded
1 tablespoon chopped fresh coriander leaves
2 teaspoons garam masala
Salt to taste

Opposite: BALTI MIXED VEGETABLE BIRIANI *(page 114),* WITH CHILLI RAITA *(page 122)*

BREADS AND RICE

Indian bread and rice take time to cook – particularly if we want both – and we may not have that time available. Although rice only takes a few minutes to cook, following a few minutes soaking, to get nice satisfying 'fluffy' grains it needs time to dry out – at least 30 minutes, better with more. One solution is to cook your rice in advance, say at the weekend, when you do have time. It will keep safely in the fridge for a day or two. Or it can be frozen then thawed overnight. Either way it is quickly re-heated by stir-frying.

Dough requires time to make (and it's messy) and if you want naan it needs more time to rise. But the actual cooking is easy enough. The results are worth it – there is nothing like fresh home-made Indian bread. Ready-made packet versions are certainly not as good, lacking that freshness, but may have to do if time is short. You will, of course, get better results for a different kind of effort: using your takeaway – and I'll turn a blind eye if needs be! Alternatively there's nothing to stop you enjoying curry with fresh crusty Western bread. Indeed cold curry makes a great sandwich filler. But that's another story. Here, meanwhile, are five Indian bread and four rice recipes which I do hope you'll find the time to make.

Opposite: BANANA FRITTERS *(page 125)*

CHAPATI

MAKES

— 4 —

INGREDIENTS

UTENSILS
*mixing bowl, tava or flat
frying-pan*
PREPARATION TIME
*20 minutes (including
15 minutes waiting)*
COOKING TIME
2 minutes

*450 g (1 lb) brown ata or
wholemeal flour (see page
19)*
Up to 1 cup water
Pinch of salt

Non-rising (unleavened) flat bread is common all over the Middle East but is best known as India's chapati. All it consists of is brown flour and water made into a pliable dough. Then it is rolled out into flat discs and dry-fried. If you are new to bread-making this is the easiest one of all. Once mastered you can progress to the other types with success guaranteed.

Chapati is usually made on a tava which is a heavy, almost flat, steel frying-pan about 20–25 cm (8–10 inches) in diameter. An ordinary large frying-pan is a suitable substitute.

In a mixing bowl, mix the flour and enough water to make a dough. Work it until it becomes an elastic, cohesive lump. Leave it for about 15 minutes. Knead the dough, then divide it into 4 and make each piece into a sphere. Roll each into a thin 10 cm (4 inch) disc. Heat a flat pan or tava to very hot. Using no oil, cook each chapati on both sides until it has no 'raw' patches and has black/brown 'blisters'. Serve hot sprinkled with a little salt.

PAN-FRIED WHITE PARATHA

M A K E S

—— 4 ——

Paratha is a large chapati, rolled out and folded over to create layers, then rolled again. It's a kind of puff pastry technique, but much much easier. It is pan-fried in ghee to make a crispy, luscious, calorie-drenched bread. Normally made from ata (chapati) flour, I'm ringing the changes here by using strong white flour.

In a mixing bowl, mix the flour and enough water to make a firm dough. Work it until it becomes an elastic lump. Leave it for about 15 minutes. Knead the dough, then divide it into 4 and make each piece into a sphere. Roll out each one as thinly as you can. Flour it, then fold it over and over as with puff pastry. Roll out again to a thin disc. Repeat this as many times as you like, the more you do it, the lighter the ultimate texture. For the final time roll out to make 18–20 cm (7–8 inch) discs. Melt some of the ghee in a frying-pan, fry a paratha on one side then the other, to a lovely golden-brown colour. Shake off excess ghee and drain on kitchen paper. Repeat with the other 3 discs and serve them hot.

INGREDIENTS

UTENSILS
**mixing bowl, large
frying-pan**
PREPARATION TIME
**25 minutes (including
15 minutes waiting)**
COOKING TIME
3–4 minutes

*750 g (1¹/₂ lb) strong white
flour*
About 1¹/₂ cups water
100 g (4 oz) butter ghee

Naan Bread

MAKES

— 4 —

UTENSILS
mixing bowl, floured board, grill pan
PREPARATION TIME
10 minutes
RISING TIME
1 hour
COOKING TIME
3 minutes

2 teaspoons fresh yeast or
1 teaspoon dried yeast or
3 tablespoons natural yoghurt
750 g (1¹/₂ lb) strong white plain flour
Up to 1¹/₂ cups lukewarm water
1 teaspoon wild onion seeds
2 tablespoons butter ghee

The traditional tandoori bread, made in the clay oven. It gets its springy fluffy texture because it is leavened (it is made to rise). This is achieved by the addition of fresh yeast (best) or dried yeast (second best) or yoghurt (least best). Given a warm place, yeast ferments, creating gas which, trapped in the dough, makes it expand and hence the bubbles in our standard loaves. After its first rising, you must 'knock back' the dough i.e. release the gas by re-kneading the dough. Practice will make perfect here, but don't give up – mastering the technique is the only way you'll get fresh as possible naan.

Dissolve the yeast (fresh or dried) in a little lukewarm water. Put the flour in a warmed bowl, make a well in the centre and pour in the yeast. Yoghurt can be used here in the absence of yeast. Gently mix into the flour and add enough warm water to make a firm dough. Remove from the bowl and knead on a floured board until well combined. Return to the bowl and leave in a warm place for an hour to rise.

Your dough, when risen, should have doubled in size. It should be bubbly, stringy and elastic. Knock back the dough by kneading it down to its original size, adding the seeds. Divide the dough into 4 equal parts. Roll each part into a tear-drop shape at least 5 mm (¹/₄ inch) thick. Pre-heat the grill to three-quarters heat, cover the grill pan with foil and set it in the midway position. Put the naan on to the foil, brush with butter ghee and grill it. Watch it cook (it can easily burn). As soon as the first side develops brown patches, remove and turn over, brush again with butter ghee and grill until it sizzles. Repeat with the other 3 naans and serve.

PESHWARI NAAN

M A K E S
—— 4 ——

No more difficult to make than naan. Simply add chopped nuts and sultanas.

Dissolve the fresh or dried yeast in a little lukewarm water. Put the flour in a warmed bowl, make a well in the centre and pour in the yeast. Yoghurt can be used here in the absence of yeast. Gently mix into the flour and add enough warm water to make a firm dough. Remove from the bowl and knead on a floured board until well combined. Return to the bowl and leave in a warm place for an hour to rise.

Your dough, when risen, should have doubled in size. It should be bubbly, stringy and elastic. Knock back the dough by kneading it down to its original size, adding the nuts, sultanas and seeds. Divide the dough into 4 equal parts. Roll each part into a tear-drop shape at least 5 mm ($^1/_4$ inch) thick. Pre-heat the grill to three-quarters heat, cover the grill pan with foil and set it in the midway position. Put the naan on to the foil, brush with butter ghee and grill it. Watch it cook (it can easily burn). As soon as the first side develops brown patches, remove and turn over, brush again with butter ghee and grill until it sizzles. Repeat with the other 3 naans and serve.

INGREDIENTS

UTENSILS
mixing bowl, floured board, grill pan
PREPARATION TIME
10 minutes
RISING TIME
1 hour
COOKING TIME
3 minutes

2 teaspoons fresh yeast or
  1 teaspoon dried yeast or
  3 tablespoons natural
  yoghurt
750 g (1$^1/_2$ lb) strong white
  plain flour
Up to 1$^1/_2$ cupfuls lukewarm
  water
25 g (1 oz) shelled, unsalted
  pistachio nuts
25 g (1 oz) golden sultanas
1 teaspoon wild onion seeds
2 tablespoons butter ghee

109

GARLIC NAAN

MAKES

—— 4 ——

UTENSILS
**mixing bowl, floured board,
grill pan**
PREPARATION TIME
10 minutes
RISING TIME
1 hour
COOKING TIME
3 minutes

*2 teaspoons fresh yeast or
1 teaspoon dried yeast or
3 tablespoons natural
yoghurt*
*750 g (1½ lb) strong white
plain flour*
*Up to 1½ cups lukewarm
water*
*1 or more garlic cloves,
crushed*
1 teaspoon wild onion seeds
2 tablespoons butter ghee

Probably not the thing to eat if you want to impress the dentist. It sure is unsociable – but it is divine and perfectly acceptable if everyone eats it.

Dissolve the fresh or dried yeast in a little lukewarm water. Put the flour in a warmed bowl, make a well in the centre and pour in the yeast. Yoghurt can be used here in the absence of yeast. Gently mix into the flour and add enough warm water to make a firm dough. Remove from the bowl and knead on a floured board until well combined. Return to the bowl and leave in a warm place for an hour to rise.

Your dough, when risen, should have doubled in size. It should be bubbly, stringy and elastic. Knock back the dough by kneading it down to its original size, add the crushed garlic and seeds. Divide the dough into 4 equal parts. Roll each part into a tear-drop shape at least 5 mm (¼ inch) thick. Pre-heat the grill to three-quarters heat, cover the grill pan with foil and set it in the midway position. Put the naan on to the foil, brush with butter ghee and grill it. Watch it cook (it can easily burn). As soon as the first side develops brown patches, remove and turn over, brush again with butter ghee and grill until it sizzles. Repeat with the other 3 naans and serve.

PLAIN RICE

There are so many different recipes for cooking rice, all claiming to achieve fluffy grains. If you already have a method which works, stick with it. If, however, your rice doesn't quite work, this method, I guarantee, will never fail to produce gorgeously fluffy, separate grains. The rice is perfectly edible the moment it is strained, but it is still quite wet. If you have the time, the real secret to achieving separate grains, is to allow 30–60 minutes for it to dry out. Rice, like lentils, absorbs water at the ratio of approximately 2:1. A single person portion of dry uncooked rice is between 60 g and 75 g (about 2 oz–3 oz) depending on appetite. After cooking and drying it swells to about 3 times in volume (rice batches vary slightly in water absorption factors, also it depends on how much polishing has been done in the factory). So the cooked rice average portion is between 185 g and 225 g (about 6½ oz–8 oz). Here then is my infallible method for cooking 'plain' rice by boiling.

――――

Pick through the rice to remove grit and impurities. Bring the water to the boil. (It is not necessary to salt it.) While it is heating up, rinse the rice briskly with fresh cold water until most of the starch is washed out. Run boiling water from the kettle through the rice at the final rinse. This minimizes the temperature reduction of the boiling water when you put the rice into it. When the water is boiling properly, put the rice into the pan. Start timing. Put the lid on the pan until the water comes back to the boil, then remove the lid. It takes 8–10 minutes from the start of timing. Stir frequently to prevent the grains sticking. After about 6 minutes, taste a few grains. As soon as the centre is no longer brittle but still has a good *al dente* bite to it, drain off the water. The rice should seem slightly undercooked. Shake off all the excess water, then place the strainer on to a dry tea towel to help remove the last of the water. After a minute place the rice in a warmed serving dish. Serve or, preferably, put the rice into a very low oven for 30–60 minutes. As it dries, the grains will separate and become fluffy.

INGREDIENTS

UTENSILS
strainer, large saucepan
PREPARATION TIME
3 minutes
COOKING TIME
8–10 minutes
DRYING TIME
30–60 minutes (optional)

225 g–350 g (8 oz–12 oz) dry uncooked basmati rice
1.2–1.75 litres (2–3 pints) water
Extra boiling water from the kettle

PULLAO RICE

S E R V E S

—— 4 ——

INGREDIENTS

UTENSILS
**strainer, medium-sized
heavy lidded saucepan or
casserole pot**
PREPARATION TIME
5 minutes
COOKING TIME
5–7 minutes
DRYING TIME
30–60 minutes (optional)

300 g (or 10 oz) basmati rice
600 ml (1 pint) water
2 tablespoons butter ghee
¹/₂ teaspoon fennel seeds
*¹/₃ teaspoon seeds of green
cardamoms*
*10 cm (4 inch) cinnamon
stick*
¹/₄ teaspoon black cumin seeds
2–3 bay leaves
2–3 star anise
1 blade mace
20–25 strands saffron
*1 tablespoon coconut milk
powder*
1 tablespoon ground almonds
Salt to taste (optional)

The famous restaurant favourite cannot be omitted from this book. The fragrance of basmati rice is enhanced with fried spices and flavourings. There is no better accompaniment to curry. And there is no better way of cooking it than by allowing it to absorb every drop of water. Here's how. It requires careful measuring of the water in the ratio 2 water:1 dry rice. Also it works much better in a heavy saucepan (or casserole pot) which holds the heat. The portion here is for average appetites. Step quantities up or down for smaller or larger appetites, and do not mix imperial (ounce) with metric (gram) measures. They are not exact conversions. Other than that it's really simple. Note the resting time (to allow the grains to go fluffy). If you're in a hurry you can omit the resting stage (see page 111).

Rinse the rice in a strainer under the cold tap for about 30 seconds. Put it into a bowl of cold water to soak for a couple of minutes. Stir to remove starch and rinse again until the water runs virtually clear. Set aside to drain. Bring the measured water to the boil in the kettle. Heat the ghee in the saucepan or casserole pot. Fry the spices for 10 seconds. Add the rice and stir-fry for a further 30 seconds. Add the boiling water. Stir and put on the lid. Lower the heat to medium. As soon as the water has absorbed into the rice (4–6 minutes) remove the pan from the heat. Stir in the coconut powder and almonds (and optional salt), and put the pan in a warm place (not direct heat) with the lid on. Leave it for between 30–60 minutes for the grains to become separated. The longer you can leave it, the better. Just before serving, fork through the rice to aerate and separate the grains.

SOUTH INDIAN RICE

SERVES

—— 4 ——

Take a batch of pre-cooked plain rice and stir-fry it with mustard seeds, coconut and cashew nuts with a squeeze of lemon juice and you have rice with a tint of sour. It's quite delicious.

———

Heat the oil in your large karahi or wok. Add the seeds and fry for 10 seconds. Add the cashew nuts and stir-fry for 1 minute. Then add the coconut and stir-fry for 10 seconds. Add the rice and stir-fry it carefully (so as not to break the grains) but rapidly to the sizzle (it will only take a couple of minutes). Stir in the tamarind or mango powder (if using) and the lemon juice, coconut powder and salt. Serve at once.

INGREDIENTS

UTENSILS
large karahi or wok
PREPARATION TIME
1 minute
COOKING TIME
3–5 minutes

Pistachio or sesame oil
1 teaspoon sesame seeds
1 teaspoon black mustard
    seeds
8–12 unsalted cashew nuts
1 tablespoon desiccated
    coconut
750 g–900 g (1$^{1}/_{2}$ lb–2 lb)
    cooked plain rice (see page
    111)
$^{1}/_{2}$ teaspoon tamarind powder
    or mango powder
    (optional)
2 tablespoons fresh lemon
    juice
1 tablespoon coconut milk
    powder
Salt to taste

BALTI MIXED VEGETABLE BIRIANI

S E R V E S

—— 4 ——

This meal in itself is so quick to make that any longer an introduction would be inappropriate.

Heat the oil. Add the curry paste, garam masala, mustard, tomato purée and ketchup, mango chutney and Worcestershire sauce. Stir-fry this mixture for 2 minutes, adding a little water to keep it mobile. Then stir-fry the vegetables and, when sizzling, add the rice. Stir-fry carefully (so as not to break the grains) until it is piping hot (about 3 more minutes). Salt to taste. Serve at once.

INGREDIENTS

UTENSILS
large karahi or wok
PREPARATION TIME
1 minute
COOKING TIME
5–6 minutes

2 tablespoons vegetable oil
1 tablespoon curry paste
2 tablespoons garam masala
$^1/_2$ teaspoon mustard powder
1 tablespoon tomato purée
1 tablespoon tomato ketchup
1 tablespoon mango chutney, chopped
1 teaspoon Worcestershire sauce
225 g (8 oz) frozen mixed vegetables, thawed
750 g (1$^1/_2$ lb) cooked plain rice (see page 111)
Salt to taste

CHUTNEYS AND ACCOMPANIMENTS

It's uncommon to find salads in India – it has a lot to do with the climate. It is so difficult, in the scorching heat, to prevent salads from going limp. The alternative for India is the instant fresh chutney. We are familiar with some of these at the restaurant – fresh onion chutney and raitas (yoghurt-based chutneys) are the best known. Not only are they nutritionally very good, they are very quick and easy to make. In my selection of recipes I have included several raitas. I happen to adore the Red Coconut Chutney and the tart Quick Lemon Pickle. The Shredded Carrot Chutney goes well with everything and hot-heads will be surprised how easy the Green Chilli Purée is to make. Any curry meal is enhanced by bottled pickles such as lime, brinjal (aubergine), mango and chilli. No quick and easy recipe for these. They take a lot of time to prepare and there are a number of good factory-made versions available, home-made taking too long to make. Bottled sweet mango chutney remains popular, but that too takes time to make at home. You might like to try my quick version.

FRESH ONION CHUTNEY

S E R V E S

—— 4 ——

INGREDIENTS

UTENSILS
small mixing bowl
PREPARATION TIME
2 minutes
COOKING TIME
nil

*100 g (4 oz) red onion,
thinly sliced*
*1 tablespoon thinly sliced red
pepper*
*6–8 fresh coriander or mint
leaves, chopped*
*¹/₂ teaspoon green chilli
(optional), chopped*
¹/₂ teaspoon garam masala
¹/₂ teaspoon paprika
Squeeze of lemon juice

To me fresh onion chutney is obligatory with any curry. Its freshness cuts through curry's richness and it is extremely good for you in health terms. Use within 48 hours or freeze to use in subsequent cooking.

Mix all the ingredients together and serve at once. You can cover and leave it in the fridge for up to 48 hours which will cause it to 'marinate' and go translucent.

TOMATO CHUTNEY

S E R V E S
—— 4 ——

A tangy, always attractive chutney which goes well with everything.

Mix all the ingredients. Chill and serve.

UTENSILS
mixing bowl
PREPARATION TIME
3 minutes
COOKING TIME
nil

12 cherry tomatoes, quartered
2–3 spring onions, chopped
5–6 fresh mint leaves, chopped
$^1/_2$ teaspoon bottled mint jelly
$^1/_3$ teaspoon wild onion seeds
1 tablespoon wine vinegar
2 teaspoons pistachio oil
Salt to taste

RED COCONUT CHUTNEY

S E R V E S
—— 4 ——

I happen to adore this chutney which is a modification of a standard South Indian chutney. It needs a tiny moment of cooking but the minimal effort is well worth it.

Heat the oil. Turn off the heat. Stir-fry the seeds and coconut for a minute. Careful here, the coconut can burn. To prevent it burning, remove it from the heat promptly and add just enough milk to make it into a thick purée texture. Mix in the chilli, tomato purée and salt to taste. Serve (or chill and serve).

UTENSILS
small karahi or wok
PREPARATION TIME
1 minute
COOKING TIME
1 minute

2 tablespoons sesame oil
1 teaspoon sesame seeds
1 teaspoon black mustard seeds
6–8 tablespoons desiccated
  coconut
Milk as required
1 fresh red chilli, chopped
1 teaspoon tomato purée
Salt to taste

QUICK MANGO CHUTNEY

S E R V E S

—— 4 ——

UTENSILS
small karahi or wok
PREPARATION TIME
2 minutes
COOKING TIME
2–2¹/₂ minutes

1 fresh sweet mango
2 tablespoons sunflower or
   soya oil
¹/₂ teaspoon mango powder
1 teaspoon paprika
¹/₂ teaspoon chilli powder
1 teaspoon curry paste
2 teaspoons vinegar (any
   type)
2 teaspoons brown sugar
¹/₂ teaspoon salt

Please don't expect the bottled version. That requires ages to cook. This uses fresh mango and but seconds of cooking – and it's a good accompaniment. Use within a day or two or freeze.

Remove the stone and scoop out and finely chop the mango pulp. Heat the oil. Fry the powders and paste for 30 seconds. Add the vinegar, sugar, salt and the mango and stir-fry for a minute or two. Cool (or chill) and serve.

Quick lemon pickle

S E R V E S

—— 4 ——

As with the previous recipe this is not like bottled lime pickle, which requires long slow cooking. This requires a short bit of cooking but it is deliciously tart and fresh and a great contrast to rich curries. If you can get them, use unwaxed lemons. Use within a day or two or freeze.

―――――

Quarter the lemons and/or limes then squeeze out their juice. Chop them into small pieces. Heat the oil, stir-fry the seeds and garlic for 20 seconds. Add the paste and mango powder and continue to stir-fry for 30 seconds. Add the juice and sugar and when it is simmering add the chopped lemon and/or lime. Stir-fry for a couple of minutes (minimum). Salt to taste, cool (or chill) and serve.

INGREDIENTS

UTENSILS
small karahi or wok
PREPARATION TIME
1–2 minutes
COOKING TIME
5 minutes

2 lemons or 4 limes (or a
  mixture), unpeeled
4 tablespoons oil
$^1/_2$ teaspoon mustard seeds
1 clove garlic, finely chopped
2 teaspoons curry paste
$^1/_2$ teaspoon mango powder
1 teaspoon sugar
Salt to taste

Shredded carrot chutney

S E R V E S

—— 4 ——

This is a tart instant chutney which is easy to make (especially if you purchase ready-shredded carrot). Use within 2 or 3 days or freeze.

―――――

Simply mix everything and serve.

INGREDIENTS

UTENSILS
small mixing bowl
PREPARATION TIME
1–2 minutes
COOKING TIME
nil

100 g (4 oz) shredded carrot
$^1/_2$ teaspoon tamarind powder
  or mango powder
$^1/_2$ teaspoon ground coriander
1 tablespoon brown sauce
1 teaspoon Worcestershire
  sauce
3–4 tablespoons red wine
  vinegar
$^1/_2$ teaspoon salt
3–4 tablespoons water

UTENSILS
small food processor
PREPARATION TIME
5 minutes
COOKING TIME
nil

20–25 fresh green cayenne
chillies, chopped
1 green pepper, chopped
150 ml (5 fl oz) vinegar (any
type)
¹/₂ teaspoon salt

Green chilli purée

M A K E S

—— 200 g (7 oz) ——

As anyone who knows me will substantiate, I always have this simple preparation in stock. It lasts indefinitely (so make a reasonable-sized batch) and goes as a chutney with many more things than curry. Beware though… it is HOT!

Put everything into the food processor. Pulse to a purée. Bottle and serve as required.

UTENSILS
lidded jar
PREPARATION TIME
1 minute
COOKING TIME
nil

300 ml (10 fl oz) vinegar
(any type)
20–30 fresh green or red
chillies

Vinegared chillies

M A K E S

—— a lot! ——

This is simplicity itself. All you have to do is put whole green or red chillies into vinegar. It solves the problem of what to do with left-over chillies. They go well with any savoury dish, such as hamburgers and kebabs, and last indefinitely. This chutney should not be given to anyone not used to chilli heat!

Choose a suitable-sized, clean lidded jar. Put the chillies in it. Fill with vinegar. Shake, top up and store until required.

RAITA

Nothing could be simpler or more effective than raita. It is yoghurt with savoury flavourings. Use thick Greek yoghurt. Requires no cooking and takes only a couple of minutes to prepare. All you need to do is mix the ingredients in a small bowl and serve. Here are six variations, all enough for four people. Use within the yoghurt's use-by date.

MILD RAITA

Delicious with any dish, especially hot ones!

INGREDIENTS

75 g (3 oz) natural Greek yoghurt
$^1/_2$ teaspoon ground coriander
Pinch of turmeric

TANDOORI RAITA

To be eaten with tandoori and tikka items and onion pakoras, or any curry dish.

INGREDIENTS

75 g (3 oz) natural Greek yoghurt
$^1/_2$ teaspoon Tandoori Paste (see page 44)
3 teaspoons bottled vinegared mint

BALTI RAITA

Good with any dish, and especially balti.

INGREDIENTS

75 g (3 oz) natural Greek yoghurt
2 teaspoons garam masala
1 teaspoon curry paste

75 g (3 oz) natural Greek
yoghurt
2.5 cm (1 inch) cucumber,
peeled and cut into
matchsticks
$^{1}/_{2}$ teaspoon garam masala

75 g (3 oz) natural Greek
yoghurt
4 fresh green or red chillies,
chopped
$^{1}/_{2}$ teaspoon chilli powder

75 g (3 oz) natural Greek
yoghurt
3 tablespoons unsweetened
desiccated coconut
$^{1}/_{2}$ teaspoon mustard seeds

CUCUMBER RAITA

The addition of cucumber matchsticks is traditional and very effective.

CHILLI RAITA

A lovely combination of the hot and the mild served cold.

COCONUT RAITA

The combination of yoghurt with the coconut is pleasant and tasty.

DESSERTS AND BEVERAGES

India's desserts and puddings are generally quite rich and sweet and they take an age to make. They are often based on milk, and they take all that time to make because someone has to stir a huge panful of milk over a gentle heat continuously to prevent sticking, until a glutinous lump of condensed milk results. This unrewarding task makes one weary just to think of it. With subsequent processing it will become fudge, ice-cream, syrup-drenched balls or some other sweet delight. Some of our Indian restaurants serve Indian sweets, but generally they are an acquired taste. Also diners are often too full to want to take on a rich and heavy pudding. The five recipes I've chosen here are neither rich nor heavy nor are they over-sugared. They are recipes which I have served over the years to thousands of people and they work well. They are quick and easy to make, and can be eaten on their own as a snack or as part of a meal. There are two beverage recipes – Indian tea (a cuppa cha – but the real thing) and Mysore coffee. The very last recipe in the book is that especially Indian invention – punch. You can enjoy that at any time of course, and when better than at the start of your cooking. Cheers!

BOMBAY SYLLABUB

S E R V E S

—— 4 ——

This is simple to make, enjoyable to eat and, believe me, it is not nearly as rich as it sounds.

Mix the yoghurt, cream and ground cardamom together in the large mixing bowl. Whisk it until it stiffens. Whisk in the sugar to taste. It should not be runny. If necessary, you can use a small quantity of ground almonds to thicken it. Chill and serve decorated with the nutmeg.

INGREDIENTS

UTENSILS
large mixing bowl, whisk
PREPARATION TIME
3–4 minutes
CHILLING TIME
2–6 hours (optional)

*600 g (1 lb 5 oz) natural
Greek yoghurt
200 ml (7 fl oz) double
cream
¹/₂ teaspoon ground cardamom
Sugar to taste
Ground almonds (if required)
Freshly grated nutmeg to
decorate*

INSTANT KULFI

S E R V E S

—— 4 ——

Kulfi is Indian ice-cream. It is harder in texture than ordinary ice-cream and usually takes an age to make. Here's my ever-so-simple instant offering.

Scoop the ice-cream into serving bowls. Sprinkle on the ground cardamom and chopped nuts and serve!

INGREDIENTS

UTENSILS
ice-cream scoop (optional)
PREPARATION TIME
30 seconds
COOKING TIME
nil

*Vanilla ice-cream
Ground cardamom
Some shelled, unsalted
pistachio nuts, chopped*

BANANA FRITTERS

S E R V E S

—— 4 ——

This used to be a popular dessert at the curry house. It seems to have dropped out of favour recently, which is a shame. These sweet fried fritters are the business. They are so good you can miss the starter and main course and have these as a snack at any time of day.

Mash the bananas with the custard powder, cornflour, coconut milk powder, egg, cardamom, salt and caster sugar to make a thick batter which will drop off the spoon, adding milk to reach the right consistency. Leave the mixture to stand for 20 minutes. Heat the ghee in the tava – a heavy, almost flat, steel frying-pan 20–25 cm (8–10 inches) in diameter – or frying-pan. Dollop 2 tablespoons of batter into the pan. Fry the fritter for a couple of minutes. Turn it over and fry the other side for a further couple of minutes, until it is crisp. To keep its shape you may have to prod the edges with a spatula. Repeat with the remaining mixture. Dust with icing sugar and serve hot with lemon wedges.

INGREDIENTS

UTENSILS
large mixing bowl, tava or large frying-pan
PREPARATION TIME
5 minutes plus 20 minutes standing
COOKING TIME
about 16 minutes

4 large, very ripe bananas
3 heaped tablespoons custard powder
2 heaped tablespoons cornflour
3 heaped tablespoons coconut milk powder
1 large egg
1 teaspoon ground green cardamom
Pinch of salt
1 tablespoon caster sugar
Milk as required
4 tablespoons butter ghee
Icing sugar for dusting
Lemon wedges to serve

QUICK INDIAN RICE PUDDING

S E R V E S

—— 4 ——

You'll need round pudding rice for this recipe. It sounds like school dinners of old, but is really delicious.

Rinse the rice in a strainer under the cold water tap, then leave it to soak while bringing 300 ml (½ pint) water to a boil in a large saucepan. Add the rice and a pinch of salt and stir from time to time. Strain after 10 minutes. Then put the condensed milk into the pan and gently heat it up. Add the drained rice, cardamom, golden syrup to taste, saffron and nuts and stir. Add a little milk if it needs thinning. Sprinkle over some nutmeg and serve hot or cold.

INGREDIENTS

UTENSILS
strainer, large saucepan
PREPARATION TIME
5 minutes
COOKING TIME
15 minutes

120 g (4¹/₂ oz) round-grain rice
Pinch of salt
2 tablespoons sweetened condensed milk
¹/₂ teaspoon ground green cardamom
1 tablespoon or more golden syrup
20 strands saffron
1 teaspoon chopped hazelnuts
Milk as required
Freshly grated nutmeg to decorate

EXOTIC FRUIT SALAD

S E R V E S

— 4 —

This is so easy and so delicious to make. I nearly always use one tin of fruit and its syrup along with the fresh fruit to speed things up and to give it a mature taste. Note also the alcoholic kick! Use whatever fresh fruit you like. Here's an example.

Open the tin of fruit and place it in the bowl with its liquid and mix in the ground cardamom and ginger (if using). Add the remaining fruit, sherry, sugar to taste. Serve chilled in stemmed glasses garnished with fresh mint leaves.

INGREDIENTS

UTENSILS
mixing bowl
PREPARATION TIME
5 minutes
CHILLING TIME
2–6 hours (optional)

200 g (7 oz) tin apricots,
  peaches or mango slices and
  their syrup
$^1/_2$ teaspoon ground green
  cardamom
2.5 cm (1 inch) piece fresh
  ginger (optional), sliced
30–40 seedless grapes (black
  or white)
1 tangerine, in segments
1 apple, peeled, cored and
  chopped
1 large banana, sliced
8·strawberries, halved
8 maraschino cherries
2–3 tablespoons sweet sherry
Caster sugar to taste
Coarsely chopped mint leaves
  to garnish

MYSORE COFFEE

SERVES
—— 4 ——

UTENSILS
your normal coffee maker
PREPARATION TIME
a few seconds
BREWING TIME
2–3 minutes

*4 × 2.5 cm (1 inch) pieces
cassia bark*
*Your normal amount of coffee
using Mysore coffee*
*¹/₂ teaspoon ground green
cardamom*

India is a coffee grower. The colourful central Indian town of Mysore is its hub. Mysore coffee is widely available, and it is of very good quality. You can take it 'straight' or try this spice-infused coffee.

Grind the cassia bark with your coffee beans or grind them and add to ready-ground coffee. Make the coffee in the way you normally do it. Add the cardamom and let them infuse for the same time as the coffee, filtering or straining them away as you serve.

INDIAN TEA

S E R V E S

—— 4 ——

My first cup of cha (or chai) in India came as a shock. The land of tea-growing doesn't make it like we do and I like tea strong, no sugar, not much milk, infused for a few minutes and hot. They like it weak, very sweet, boiled in milk for 10 minutes with spices and lukewarm! Actually, it's delicious. Try it with an open mind and I'm sure you'll agree.

Put everything into the saucepan. Heat and then maintain a gentle simmer for 10 minutes. Extract and discard the tea bags. Serve with 1 cardamom and 1 cinnamon stick per portion.

INGREDIENTS

UTENSILS
large saucepan
PREPARATION TIME
1 minute
COOKING TIME
12 minutes

2 tea bags
600 ml (1 pint) milk
3 tablespoons unsweetened
   evaporated milk
2 tablespoons sugar
4 × 10 cm (4 inch) cinnamon
   sticks
4 green cardamoms

PUNCH

UTENSILS
large saucepan
PREPARATION TIME
1–2 minutes
COOKING TIME
nil

*150–300 ml (5–10 fl oz)
water (optional)
4 cloves, crushed
4 green cardamoms, crushed
4 × 10 cm (4 inch) cinnamon
sticks
1 tablespoon fresh lemon or
lime juice
1 tablespoon brown sugar
750 ml (1¹/₄ pints) sweetish
white wine (such as
Sauternes)
50 ml (2 fl oz) schnapps or
brandy
Sprigs of mint to garnish
(optional)*

They say you should save the best till last and go out with a bang! And so we shall! Well not 'out' literally I hope, but here's my alcoholic finale which you can use to welcome guests, to accompany a meal, to help the cooking, as a nightcap or at any time. It's appropriate, too, because punch is an Indian invention. It derives its name from the Hindi word panch meaning five, because five ingredients were used: arrack (potent spirit), sugar, lime juice, spice and water. The British Raj soon cottoned on and devised many ways of making punch but I see no reason why we shouldn't enjoy it more or less the original Indian way. In place of arrack I've used sweet white wine and schnapps or brandy. It is delightful warm or iced. Add the maximum quantity of water only if you want a more diluted punch.

Bring the water, cloves, cardamom and the cinnamon to the simmer in a large saucepan. Add the lemon or lime juice, sugar and the wine and schnapps or brandy. Turn off the heat and serve when cool enough to drink. Or let it cool and add ice. Either way serve with the cloves and cardamom removed but the cinnamon stick retained in tall glasses. Garnish with mint sprigs if you like.

MENUS

These are just examples of dishes which go well together at different times of day and for different occasions. From brunch to feast, and picnic to party, you'll always find something in this book which suits and pleases. And it's not all light snacks and quick preparations. Using only a selection of the recipes, and allowing the time, you can create the ultimate: a splendid dinner party. My 'Festive Occasion' menu gives 8 people an impressive 5-course banquet. Not only will you be the talk of the town, you'll be really satisfied with the achievement.

Unless otherwise stated, all menus serve 4 people. You can of course amend the amounts of ingredients proportionately to suit the number of people.

ANY TIME SNACK

In Under 15 Minutes
Vegetable Curry Bap (p. 30)
Mild Raita (p. 121)

SPICY BRUNCH

In Under 15 Minutes
Curried Scrambled Egg (p. 35)
Tomato Chutney (p. 117)
Crusty French Bread

A LIGHT LUNCH

In 20 Minutes
Curried Crab Chowder (p. 41)
Pan-fried Curried Fish (p. 86)
Re-heated Plain Rice (p. 111)

AFTERNOON TEA SNACK

In Under 25 Minutes
Banana Fritters (p. 125)
Indian Tea (p. 129)

A SNACK OR SUPPER

In 25 Minutes
Cumin-flavoured Liver Stir-Fry (p. 38)
Chapati (p. 106)
Quick Lemon Pickle (p. 119)

A TV DINNER

In $1^1/_2$ hours (mostly waiting for the oven)
Grilled Spicy Lamb Chops (p. 58)
Tandoori Baked Potato (p. 50)
Coconut Raita (p. 122)
Salad

SUNDAY LUNCH

In 45 Minutes
Herbal Chicken Curry (p. 73)
Cauliflower Bhajee (p. 92)
South Indian Rice (p. 113)
Fresh Onion Chutney (p. 116)

Bombay Syllabub (p. 124)

A TANDOORI MIXED GRILL

Suitable For 6–8 People
Sheek Kebabs (p. 46)
Tandoori Boneless Chicken (p. 48)
Tandoori King Prawns (p. 49)
Tandoori Baked Potato (p. 50)
Garlic Naan (p. 110)
Tandoori Raita (p. 121)
Green Salad

A SPICY PICNIC

All served cold
Kashmiri Mushroom and Fennel (p. 37)
Potatoes in a Pickly Sauce (p. 39)
Tandoori Avocado Crab (p. 54)
Meat Tikka (p. 51)
Butter Prawns (p. 32)
Balti Mixed Vegetable Biriani (p. 114)

Exotic Fruit Salad (p. 127)

A SOUTH INDIAN VEGETARIAN CURRY MEAL

South Indian Vegetable Curry (p. 99)
Tarka Dhal (p. 101)
South Indian Rice (p. 113)
Chutneys (p. 116–9)

A NORTH INDIAN VEGETARIAN CURRY MEAL

Spicy Spinach with Cottage Cheese (p. 96)
Bean and Chilli Masala (p. 98)
Chapati (p. 106)
Chutneys (p. 116–9)

A THREE-COURSE DINNER

Crispy Cold Snack (p. 36)

Balti Beef with Chick Peas and Spinach (p. 57)
Peshwari Naan (p. 109)
Balti Raita (p. 121)

Quick Indian Rice Pudding (p. 126)

A FOUR-COURSE DINNER

Mulligatawny Soup (p. 40)

Prawn and Mushroom Tikka Stir-fry (p. 53)

Thai Pork Green Curry (p. 66)
Spicy Courgette and Mangetout Jal-frezi (p. 94)
Plain Rice (p. 111)
Red Coconut Chutney (p. 117)

Instant Kulfi (p. 124)

A FESTIVE OCCASION

Five Courses for up to 8 Diners

Plan ahead and cook ahead where possible (use fridge or freezer if possible). Allow 3 hours kitchen time on the day. For 8 diners, double up the punch, fritters, prawn cocktail, rice, desserts and coffee quantities given in the recipes.

Punch (p. 130)
Onion Fritters (p. 31)

Tandoori Prawn Cocktail (p. 47)

Chicken Tikka Masala (p. 75)
Balti Sweetcorn, Celery and Peas (p. 97)
Tarka Dhal (p. 101)
Pullao Rice (p. 112)
Shredded Carrot Chutney (p. 119)
Cucumber Raita (p. 122)
Pan-fried White Paratha (p. 107)

Exotic Fruit Salad (p. 127)

Mysore Coffee (p. 128)

INDEX

Entries in *italic* refer to illustrations

A

Aloo gobi curry	102
Ata	9
Aubergine	16
spicy mashed	95
Avocado crab, tandoori	54

B

Balti	
beef with chick peas and spinach	57
chicken and mushroom curry	72
mixed vegetable biriani	*103*, 114
pan	13
raita	121
sweetcorn, celery and peas	97
Banana fritters	*104*, 125
Basil	16
Bay leaf (*tej patia*)	21
Bean and chilli masala	98
Beef, with chick peas and spinach	57
Besan	18–19
Bhajee, cauliflower	92
Biriani, balti mixed vegetable	*103*, 114
Blender	13, 14
Bombay	
pomfret	85
potato	100
syllabub	124
Breads	105
chapati	106
garlic naan	110
naan	108
pan-fried white paratha	*70*, 107
Peshwari naan	*33*, 109
Butter prawns	32
with Peshwari nan	*33*

C

Cardamon (*burra and hare elaichi*)	21, 24
Carrot chutney, shredded	*69*, 119
Casserole pot	12–13
Cassia bark (*dalchini*)	22
Cauliflower bhajee	92
Chapati	106
Chicken	
boneless tandoori	48
herbal curry	73
Madras	76
Malayan	74
minced, curry	77
and mushroom, balti	72
tikka	52
with pullao rice	*34*
tikka masala	75
Chillies	16, 21
green purée	120
raita	*103*, 122
vinegared	120
Chowder, curried crab	41
Chapati flour	19
Chutneys and accompaniments	115–22
fresh onion chutney	116
green chilli purée	120
quick lemon pickle	119
quick mango chutney	118
raita	*68*, 121–2
red coconut chutney	117
shredded carrot chutney	*69*, 119
tomato chutney	*67*, 117
vinegared chillies	120
Cinnamon (*dalchini chino*)	22, 24
Clove (*lavang*)	21–2, 24
Coconut	20
chutney	117
raita	122
Cod tikka masala	83

D

Coffee	
grinder	13
Mysore	128
Coriander (*dhania*)	22, 24
leaf	16–17
Courgette and mangetout jal-frezi	*69*, 94
Crab	
chowder, curried	41
and shrimp curry	88
tandoori avocado	54
Crispy cold snack	36
Cucumber raita	*68*, 122
Cumin (*kala jeera*)	22, 24
Cumin-flavoured liver stir-fry	38
Curry paste mixture	27

D

Dhal, tarka	101
Deep-fryer	14
Desserts and beverages	123–30
banana fritters	125
Bombay syllabub	124
exotic fruit salad	127
Indian tea	129
instant kulfi	124
Mysore coffee	128
punch	130
quick Indian rice pudding	126
Duck, Rajasthani curry	79

E

Egg curry with sweetcorn	80
Egg plant *see* Aubergine	
Eggs, curried scrambled	35
Exotic fruit salad	127

F

Fennel (soonf) 22–3
Fenugreek (methi) 23
Fish and seafood 81–90
  baked spicy red mullet 68, 87
  Bombay pomfret 85
  cod tikka masala 83
  crab and shrimp curry 88
  Goan fragrant red prawn curry 89
  grilled spicy rainbow trout 84
  king prawn chilli masala 90
  lemon sole mouli 82
  pan-fried curried fish 86
Flour 18–19
Food processor 13, 14
Fresh onion chutney 116
Fritters
  banana 104, 125
  onion 31
Fruit salad, exotic 127

G

Garam masala 28
Garlic 17
  naan 110
  powder, ground 25
Ginger 18
Goan fragrant red prawn curry 89
Gram flour 18–19
Green chilli purée 120

H

Heat 9
Herbal
  chicken curry 73
  rasam soup 42
Hot hotter hottest curry 61–3

I

Indian tea 129
Instant kulfi 124

J

Jal-frezi
  courgette and mangetout 69, 94
  herbal chicken 73
Jardaloo boti 65

K

Karahi 13
  stir-fried meat with green herbs 60
Kashmiri mushroom and fennel 37
Kebabs, sheek 46
King prawns
  chilli masala 90
  tandoori 49
Korma, traditional aromatic lamb 56
Kulfi, instant 124

L

Lamb
  grilled spicy chops 58
  traditional aromatic korma 56
Lemon pickle 119
Lemon sole mouli 82
Lentils 19
Liver, cumin flavoured stir-fry 38
Lovage (ajwain) 23

M

Mace (javitri) 23
Madras
  chicken 76
  curry 61
Malayan chicken 74
Mango 17
  chutney 118
  powder (amchur) 25
Marinade, tandoori 45
Masala
  bean and chilli 98
  chicken tikka 75
  cod tikka 83
  king prawn chilli 90
Measures 9
Meat
  moghlai 64, 67
  stir-fried karahi with green
    herbs 60
  tikka 51
Meat curries 56–66
  balti beef with chick peas and
    spinach 57
  green Thai pork 66
  hot, hotter, hottest 61–3
  karahi meat with green herbs 60
  lamb chops 58
  lamb korma 56
  Madras 61
  meat with fruit and nuts 65
  meat moghlai 64, 67
  pasanda, pan-fried 59
  phal 63
  vindaloo 62
Menus 131–3
Mild raita 121
Minced chicken curry 77
Miniature food processor 14
Mint 17
Mixed vegetable biriani 103, 114
Moghlai, meat 64
  with tomato chutney 67
Mouli, lemon sole 82
Mullet, red 68, 87
Mulligatawny soup 40
Mushroom and fennel, Kashmiri 37
Mustard (rai) 23
Mysore coffee 128

N

Naan bread 108
  garlic 110
  Peshwari 33, 109
Nutmeg (jaifal) 23

O

Oils 19
Okra 17
  with mangetout, pan-fried 93
Onion 18
  chutney 116
  fritters 31

P

Pao Bhajee 30
Paprika 25
Paratha, white pan-fried 70, 107
Pasanda, pan-fried 59
Pepper, black (kala mirch) 23
Peshwari naan 109
  and butter prawns 33
Phal curry 63
Pickle, lemon 119
Plain rice 111
Pomfret, Bombay 85
Pork, Thai green curry 66
Portions 9
Potatoes
  Bombay 100
  in a pickly sauce 39
  tandoori baked 50
Poultry and eggs 71–80

balti chicken and mushroom
   curry — 72
chicken tikka masala — 75
egg curry with sweetcorn — 80
herbal chicken curry — 73
Madras curry — 76
Malayan chicken — 74
minced chicken curry — 77
Rajasthani duck curry — 79
Thai red fragrant turkey curry — 78
Prawn
   butter — 32
   cocktail, tandoori — 47
   Goan red prawn curry — 89
   king prawn chilli masala — 90
   and mushroom tikka stir-fry — 53
   tandoori king prawns — 49
Preparation — 10, 11
Pullao rice — 112
   with chicken tikka — *34*
Punch — 130
Purée, green chilli — 120

R

Rainbow trout, grilled — 84
Raita — *68*, 121–2
Rajasthani duck curry — 79
Rasam soup, herbal — 42
Red coconut chutney — 117
Red mullet, baked — *68*, 87
Rice — 19, 105
   plain — 111
   pudding — 126
   pullao — *34*, 112
   South Indian — 113

S

Saffron (*zafran or kasar*) — 23
Sag paneer — 96
Saucepans — 12
Scrambled eggs, curried — 35
Sheek kebabs — 46
Shredded carrot chutney — 119
Snacks and titbits — 29–32, 35–42

butter prawns — 32
crispy cold snack — 36
cumin-flavoured liver stir-fry — 38
curried crab chowder — 41
curried scrambled eggs — 35
herbal rasam soup — 42
Kashmiri mushroom and fennel — 37
mulligatawny soup — 40
onion fritters — 31
potatoes in a pickly sauce — 39
vegetable curry bap — 30
Soups
   herbal rasam — 42
   mulligatawny — 40
South Indian
   rice — 113
   vegetable curry — 99
Spices — 20–6
   containers — 14
   mill — 14
Spinach with cottage cheese — *70*, 96
Star anise (*chakra phool*) — 24
Stir-fry
   cumin-flavoured liver — 38
   karahi meat with green herbs — 60
   prawn and mushroom tikka — 53
Sweetcorn, celery and peas, balti — 97
Syllabub, Bombay — 124

T

Tamarind powder (*imli*) — 25
Tandoori — 43
   avocado crab — 54
   baked potato — 50
   boneless chicken — 48
   king prawns — 49
   marinade — 45
   paste — 44
   prawn cocktail — 47
   raita — 121
Tarka dhal — 101
Tea, Indian — 129
Thai
   pork green curry — 66
   red fragrant turkey curry — 78
Tikka — 43

chicken — 52
chicken masala — 75
cod masala — 83
meat — 51
prawn and mushroom stir-fry — 53
Tinned items — 20
Tomato chutney — *67*, 117
Trout, grilled rainbow — 84
Turkey, red fragrant curry — 78
Turmeric (*haldi*) — 25

U

Utensils — 12–14

V

Vegetable
   biriani, mixed — *103*, 114
   curry, South Indian — 99
   curry bap — 30
Vegetables — 10
Vegetables and lentils — 91–102
   aloo gobi curry — 102
   balti sweetcorn, celery and peas — 97
   bean and chilli masala — 98
   Bombay potato — 100
   cauliflower bhajee — 92
   pan-fried okra with mangetout — 93
   South Indian vegetable curry — 99
   spicy courgette and mangetout
      jal-frezi — *69*, 94
   spicy mashed aubergine — 95
   spicy spinach with cottage
      cheese — *70*, 96
   tarka dhal — 101
Vindaloo curry — 62
Vinegared chillies — 120

W

White flour — 19
White paratha, pan-fried — *70*, 107
Wild onion seeds (*kalonji*) — 24